The Country Dance Book

THE OLD COUNTRY DANCE

The Country Dance Book

*The Best of the
Early Contras & Squares
Their History, Lore, Callers,
Tunes & Joyful Instructions*

By Beth Tolman *&* Ralph Page

Illustrations by F. W. P. Tolman

The Stephen Greene Press

BRATTLEBORO · VERMONT

With grateful acknowledgment to *Yankee* Magazine in which some of the dance material first appeared, and to the Country Dance and Song Society of America for their help in the preparation of the new 1976 edition. And a special word of thanks to Norm Rogers who brought this lovely book to our attention in the first place.

The original edition was designed by Vrest Orton and published in 1937 by The Countryman Press, Inc.

This book has been produced in the United States of America.

It is published by The Stephen Greene Press, Brattleboro, Vermont 05301

Library of Congress Cataloging in Publication Data

Tolman, Beth.
    The country dance book.
    Summary: An authentic collection of over 75 contra square dances, their origins and lore and how to dance them.
    Includes index.
    1. Square dancing. 2. Square dance music. 3. Country-dance. 4. Country-dances. I. Page, Ralph, 1903-   joint author. II. Title.
GV1763.T6 1976   793.3'4   75-41877
ISBN 0-8289-0273-9
ISBN 0-8289-0274-7 pbk.

Contents

List of Illustrations

The Country Dance Book

LADIES GRAND CHAIN

Author's Note

A WORD IN HONOR OF

THE NEW 1976 EDITION

A lot of dancing feet have gone up and down the center since the first edition of *The Country Dance Book* came off the presses in 1937. At that time we really believed that everybody in the country knew how to dance a contra dance. How naive can you be? Very likely few even knew how to do a proper "square." And, for those of you who are newcomers to country dance, right here might be a good spot to get our terms straight. Later on, Chapter V offers a quick rule of thumb: *contry,* or contra, dances plus *quadrilles,* or squares, equal *country.* An early look at this easy formula should help clear the air.

Bicentennial celebrations have aroused a tremendous surge in the older dance forms of our nation, and the desire to learn and to dance the dances of our forefathers—and especially the contras (our particular favorites)—is a source of much gratification to many of us old-timers.

Interest in the more familiar modern "square"

dance has developed rather steadily and rather
rapidly over the years and these dances now enjoy a
widespread following; but the contra dances survived
in the United States chiefly because of the many
"islands" of interest scattered around the country,
especially in northern New England. One of these
"islands" was our home town of Nelson, New Hampshire, and the nearby towns of Stoddard, Hancock,
Antrim and Harrisville. Here we continued dancing
Hull's Victory, Money Musk, Chorus Jig, Lady
Walpole's Reel, Fisher's Hornpipe, and Plain Quadrilles, along with an occasional waltz or galop. At
the time we didn't realize that we were keeping
traditional dances alive. We danced them because we
liked them.

Another reason for their survival was the fact
that scores of musicians lived in the area who were
capable of playing the correct music for them. Levi
Messer, Romy Farr, Al Quigley, Russ Allen and
Dick Richardson were fiddlers of the highest order.
When any one of them was playing lead fiddle you
knew that the correct music for any contra dance you
wanted was only for the asking.

What is the status of country dance today? In
square dance clubs all over the country—and there
are literally thousands of them (see the current information on country dance societies and square
dance clubs at the back of this new edition)—it is
becoming the "in" thing to learn and dance some of
the older traditional dances, especially the contra
dances. You will find them being danced in modern-
day square dance clubs from Maine to California

and from Minnesota to Texas on a more or less regular basis, a few of them at each meeting of the club. True, modern square dance clubs dance more of the newer complicated dances of the day, but the fact that they dance traditional dances at all is a sure sign of a growing interest in early country dance— and something to be proud of. At the same time, the number of traditional dance societies that have long kept the old steps alive continues to swell. Certainly country dance in 1976 is on the wax.

You might also ask has the music changed? Well, yes and no. Modern square dances are danced to tunes of the day. Nobody should find fault with that: that has been the way since time immemorial. The contras are still danced pretty much to the same kind of music that they have always been danced to. Once in a while you will hear some local fiddler trying his hand at fitting his favorite blue-grass fiddle tunes to a contra. It isn't the best combination in the world. Lost, perhaps forever, are the wonderful full-band orchestrations for Plain Quadrilles such as "Prince of Good Fellows," "The Black Cat," "Circus," "Autumn Leaves," etc. Lost, too, are the old-time Quadrille Bands consisting of first and second violins, cello, contra bass, viola, first and second cornets, first and second clarinets, trombone and tuba, with sometimes a flute and piano. Perhaps the current resurgence of interest in the older dance forms will eventually include an interest in the dance orchestras of former years.

And, as the music has changed, so have some of the calls. Set a modern square dance buff loose in the glossary of calls found in Chapter II and he would likely get mighty befuddled, even though the patterns are ones that he follows time and time again under different names. Even the traditional dance buff might find some of the calls strange to his ears: time and miles have played their part.

To end on a more personal note, I became a full-time professional square dance caller in 1938, just one year after this book was first published. Since then I have called and taught New England dances all over the United States and Canada, as well as in Japan where the sponsor was the U.S. Department of State's Exchange of Persons Branch, and in England sponsored by the English Folk Dance and Song Society.

Yes, a lot of dancing feet have gone up and down the center since the first edition of *The Country Dance Book*. Beth Tolman joins me in hoping that maybe yours will be counted in before the next.

RALPH PAGE
Keene, New Hampshire
January, 1976

THE COUNTRY DANCE

*WHEREIN WE "BOW TO THE
YOUNGEST AND SALUTE THE OLDEST"*

Chapter I

JUST how much are we enjoying the jigs, reels, quadrilles and hornpipes that used to rollick all America back in its teens? Who does the country dances now, and where? Why are they, or why aren't they, still being done in your town and our town? These are questions to be answered in lots of ways, depending, of course, upon what section of the country you hail from.

Giving you the picture of our own town, Nelson, New Hampshire, the answer goes something like this: We, villagers and visitors, young and old, dance the country dances every Saturday night in the old town hall. Why? Because we've always danced them—for one hundred and seventy years; because there are plenty of available musicians who have

7

grown up in the purple of the country dance tradition; because we have an inspiring caller; and because there is always somebody coming along eager to join in, thus adding new faces and feet to our Saturday good times.

We'd rather shake down a Hull's Victory, or pop a large specimen through to the measures of Pop Goes the Weasel, than do all your slithery Four Hundreds in all your dancing dives in the United States. And, they say that throughout Vermont, villages too reduced in number to support a full-fledged country dance at regular intervals, rather than do the moderns, prefer to assemble occasionally at each other's houses for informal "junkets." (You remember the kitchen junket in *The Old Homestead*, don't you?)

But hold on; just because that's how it is in our town and in certain towns in Vermont, don't get the idea that it must be the same throughout every rural section of our land.

Take the case of a town not more than fifteen miles away from us, for instance. We're willing to bet that if you mentioned a Morning Star or a Portland Fancy, the villagers would smile just as they would if you spoke in a contemporary way of tin peddlers, red flannel ankle-lengths, or dried apples in the attic. It's a sad situation, isn't it, but probably as natural to that town ("whose name shall be X") as our situation is to us. X happens not to have any local musicians; many of its people are too churchy

1976 note: The reader should remember throughout that *The Country Dance Book* was first written in 1937.

to countenance even the mention of the word dance; and there are few city folks there who have had the experience to initiate a country dance if they wanted to.

Now take Dearborn and Storrowton where Henry Ford and Mrs. Storrow have poured out their energies and money to create two lovely New England villages in the old tradition. A dozen years ago Mr. Ford did much to re-awaken slumbering interest in the country dance. (Remember Mellie Dunham?) Today at both these places country dancing is enjoyed at least once a week by an ever-increasing crowd.

And as a variation on the same theme: there are lots of isolated "islands" throughout the United States where certain enterprising ones have rescued the country dances much as they would pluck a fine old handicraft out of near-oblivion, collect wooden implements our forefathers used, or do any one of a hundred things that would rate approval from the local Historical Society. There is much to be said for the fine loyalty of these people, their devotion to keeping another "quaint" American custom in repair, even though at times we want to guffaw at these earnest and perspiring ones as they go through their bi-weekly renditions of the Varsovienne and Downeast Breakdown. Hats off, anyway, to them all . . . these people are the worthy recorders of the tribe's ways, and it is due to them alone that many of our old things are more than mere memories today.

Just how many Nelsons, how many towns like X,

1976 note: Country dance is still performed at Storrowton, now a part of the Eastern States Exposition Grounds at West Springfield, Massachusetts.

how many Dearborns and Storrowtons there are, it is hard to say. More and more as we go about we are finding towns like our own town; more and more we are coming across such grand encouragements as the annual competition and exhibit at Durham, New Hampshire, in Farmers' Week, the seven-day fair of the New Hampshire League of Arts and Crafts, Mr. and Mrs. Ira Kent's cup tournament in Calais, Vermont, every summer, or the fine country dance show at the Eastern States Exposition in Springfield, Massachusetts.

We wish we had an airplane view of the whole country. But being provincial Yankees, we can be only like the frog that hollers for his own puddle. So, what you read here is purely out of our personal experience . . . what our ears and eyes have told us and what our grandmothers and grandfathers have passed on to us in their reminiscences of the good old days. We don't pretend, then, that this book will turn out to be a scholarly thesis on the dance . . . there must be some of these already in print . . . nor do we dare hope that it will be a quotable authority. All we want is that you and you and you will find something representative in these accounts, something helpful to your own situation, be it trying to replant the country dance seed again in fallow soil, or keeping the plant alive amid the storm and high wind of today's diversions.

As we say, we are finding encouraging signs most everywhere we go. In some places the country dance interest has reached such a height that we're willing to bet many of the town halls will soon bust their seams, or rock so rhythmically one Saturday night that the old spring floors will go the way of Jericho's walls!

In other places, once-, or twice-removed Yanks who have seen some of the swell dancing done by Fair groups and others, have become anxious themselves to learn to do the dances of their grandparents; and many have wisely engaged a prompter, a fiddler, piano player, and a nucleus of experienced dancers to teach them their ABC's.

And not only is encouragement to be found in the dancing field. All over the lot we find the young boys and girls playing the old-time music, many of them in a more modern idiom: playing tag with the notes, or improvising a bit of jazz here and there. As horrified as some of the orthodox old-timers may be, we believe this is a terribly encouraging note, for how else than by suiting a thing to its present-day needs, can we hope to keep its tradition really alive and meaningful? Later on, we shall see examples of this adaptation of the music and dances to the needs of different eras and localities. Always, of course, the rear-guard of oldsters have sent up their groans over what really was no more than a step in the natural evolution of the country dance. These old folks keep forgetting that they, as youngsters, were the very ones who changed and adapted the figures of some dance or other more nearly to suit their own needs! But that's the way it always is in every field, be it building, diet or morals.

Now that we have taken a cursory look at the present, let's glance back some generations . . . for how can we completely appreciate today if we aren't willing to consider yesterday and the day before? We speak, remember, only for New England, and then, only from our own section of the seats. But since our local stories can doubtless be duplicated in, or applied to, other sections of New England, so it seems that New England's story is at least partly representative of much of the United States.

New England, as we all know, is one of the oldest corners of our country. It is compact, integrated and, comparatively speaking, it loves its traditions. Here is a coast settlement that has experienced a constant injection of lusty immigrants fresh from dancing on their own village greens. If ever a people were given a chance to be born and bred in the purple of their dances, the Yanks were those people. As babies they were often lulled to rest to the measures of Speed The Plow or Smash The Window; and often they were carried to an assembly or junket where they were cradled in communal beds made from benches, seat to seat arrangement. Way before they were out of their swaddling clouts, then, these kids must have understood what was what on the dance floor. Then at an early age they began doing the dances themselves; later the stern dancing masters polished their steps and taught them how to "make manners" on the dance floor. What a foundation!

In "those days," dancing was the pet amusement. Seeing such a surprising number of non-dancing, non-card playing (that doesn't exclude Beano, however!) Yankees in our country towns today, we may be led to believe that the Puritans deemed a dance floor the symbol of eternal wickedness. But no, darned if they didn't think just the opposite! They encouraged the practice with the typically Puritan justification that "it promotes grace and an erect carriage." In certain localities, however, and during certain times, dancing *was* banned.

During the Revolutionary years everybody danced, including the minister, who found his place in the community via an Ordination Ball rather than by any such dour celebrations as are common today. As a minister, he was judged less by his pulpit pratings than by his ability to hold his Old Medford and handle a difficult figure. The officers in both the English troops and the Colonials were so crazy about dancing that some say, if you listen hard enough, the hills of New England will give forth a faint echo of Lord Howe's revels, or perhaps let go a few strains of Washington's favorite, Sir Roger de Coverly.

All over New England, tavern vied with tavern

for the dancers' favor, some going so far as to provide
carriages for the more distinguished guests. Michael
Whidden's Inn, over here in Portsmouth, New
Hampshire, was famous throughout New England
for its lavish assemblies (current name for country
dance shindigs). Can you picture one of these affairs
with the two floor managers in powdered wigs and
bright apparel, hat under arm, meeting each lady at
the door and sweeping her onto the dance floor?
Leading out the eldest lady present, or a bride, if
one happened to be there, these gaudy gallivanters
would start off with a Grand March of their own
choice. About ten o'clock lunch would be due . . .
cold meat sandwiches, sangaree lemonade and scald-
ing hot chocolate. If it was a holiday, the lunch
would be postponed until eleven-thirty, when the
dining hall doors opened wide to a spread of turkey,
venison or oysters. Promptly at a quarter past twelve
the dance would begin again, to run until the
break-up at dawn.

Early in the nineteenth century, people began their
dances much earlier, especially on Thanksgiving,
New Year's, or the Fourth of July. Gathering at
town halls and other places at two in the afternoon,
they would at once jump into the thing with both
feet and keep going until morning, or until the cider
and cinnamon ran out! Can you imagine such an
affair, nobody ruffled by the prospect of another hard
day at the plow or the churn? Think of us today in
that light! If the oldsters but knew, they would turn

handsprings in their graves and lament the passing of a strong race. All we can manage are some four hours of dancing, with slip-shod, easy-going modern shuffles thrown in as respite! What weaklings we are, we who compare these few hours between the first quadrille and Home Sweet Home to a morning's workout in the wood-shed!

Scheduled affairs, however, were not the only ones Yankees enjoyed then, anymore than today, for when the dancing mood took people, there was no remedy but to dance.

Some of the larger farmhouses had dance rooms built right in along the back of the second story (you can identify them often today). But most of the modest farmhouses made no special provision for a dance. So they just used the kitchen! Everything got cleared away for the affair . . . even the stove if the kitchen was small! Into the sink the fiddler-prompter would swing, and sitting there in state, he'd scrape and call an evening's fun.

Invitations to these junkets (sometimes known as heel-burners) were as casual and individual as the affairs themselves. The way they used to do it in Munsonville, New Hampshire, was like this: someone would get up on the steps of the General Store and bellow JUNKET! JUNKET! to the east, west, north and south. We've always had fun imagining the effect . . . you've seen sea-gulls swarm to a spot hitherto innocent of life? That's what the gathering of the junketeers always reminded us of.

Later it became the custom to print junket invitations on the backs of playing cards (in the days when cards were blank on one side). So, had you lived at that particular time, you might well have found an Ace of Spades under your door, backed with: "Eben Sawyer requests the favor of your company at a dance in his house on Sawyer Hill, Friday evening next, seven o'clock, January 14, 1819."

If the place was some distance from the Center, everybody tumbled into a hayrick at the store, or, if winter time, into a sleigh behind a pair of steers to drive over the unbroken snowy roads.

When quadrilles were danced at these junkets the music was usually jigs, reels or even popular songs; very seldom was straight quadrille music used. The Girl I Left Behind Me, When Johnnie Comes Marching Home, Marching Through Georgia, were common songs in grannie's day . . . in fact, they were recent enough hits so that the fiddler was always sure of double appreciation whenever he played them. So, you will see when we come to the chapter on quadrilles that the modern tendency to use other than quadrille music for quadrilles is no more than an outgrowth of the junket preference.

Every time we think of junkets we are reminded of a family story about one John Thomas. Thomas was a southerner who had moved up with his family to Wood's Mill, near Stoddard, New Hampshire, right after the Civil War. While the family were tolerated by their neighbors, naturally enough they weren't received with open arms. Thomas was a pleasure-loving man, and it hurt him very much not to be included in the kitchen junkets going on all about him. One time, though, Thomas and his wife did arrive on their own initiative, in the midst of a kitchen party nearby. "Why, Mr. Thomas," the quick-witted hostess said, "I have just this minute handed my husband a note to take over to you, asking you folks to come." Thomas, just as quick-witted, replied: "Well, thank you, ma'am, we 'lowed there was one out for us, so we just come along." All during our growing-up years we liked to think that that kitchen junket was responsible for patching up a tiny bit of the unbrotherly feeling rife at that time.

Huskings, raisings, sugaring-offs, sheep-shearings and weddings, too, of course, were incomplete without a fiddler to put everyone in the right mood.

In Vermont and down the Connecticut River Valley, and way down in Nantucket, the communal sheep-shearing was a rousing excuse for a big dance. For years it seemed that Nantucket was the meeting place of the fastest shearers, the shrewdest peddlers and the best dancers. As you can imagine, this combination always guaranteed success for the Sheep-Shearers' Ball which lasted a week there and was talked about, justifiably, for all the next year. And when Jeremiah Story of Hopkinton, New Hampshire, raised his two-story house, the neighbors celebrated the event by a party. Everybody, including Jeremiah himself, who was a hundred and one years old, boasted that he danced every figure right through until "the morning pried up the sun with a crowbar."

In the old days certain tunes went with certain dances and were never separated, and nothing exasperates the old-timers more than to have the opposite of this sometimes hold today. They can bear the quickened tempo if it doesn't allow them to show off their fanciest steps, but they cannot abide the wrong music played for a dance. Most of the modern orchestras still play the corresponding tunes to Hull's Victory, Money Musk, Pop Goes the Weasel or Chorus Jig, but for Morning Star or Lady Walpole's Reel . . . those perennial favorites . . . the more different tunes played while the dances are in progress, the better it suits the young people. The older folk are different. One old Yankee of no mean fiddling and pigeon's wing ability once told us that he could no more dance or play a hornpipe to The Bonnet Trimmed in Blue or a Pat'nella to Go Aisy, Annie, than he could harrow his oatfield with a hayrake.

Orthodoxy surely was the note in the old dancing days. Dancing masters who taught the rules with a birch-rod authority were as much a part of every community as the minister. In college towns many of the professors augmented their meager salaries by opening dancing academies. In the more populated towns they usually taught three days a week: Ladies, 9 to 12 A.M. and the Gentlemen, 5 to 8 P.M. After the first month the two groups usually combined and received joint instruction.

In the smaller villages where there was no permanent dancing master, the junkets and town hall gatherings were supplemented by itinerant dancing masters who taught many a gangling farm kid to cut a pigeon's wing before he was out of his teens.

After the rules were digested, the dancing master would proceed with instructions in the quadrille and minuet steps, and from these to the popular contry dances of the day. Some of the names of these early contrys sound strange to our ears now: Old Father George, Orange Tree, High Betty Martin, Rolling Hornpipe, Constancy, The President, Priest's House, Leather Strap, Lady Bartlett's Whim and Petty-coatee.

Dancing school niceties, however, were frequently tarnished by the practical jokes which young smart-alecks always like to play. The old stand-by was an injection of something smelly in the stove. The dancers would be put to rout, of course, and wouldn't be able to return until the stench had burned itself out and the hall had been aired and re-heated. This was an orthodox stunt at Election Day balls and Victory dances, perpetrated usually by those who had backed the losing candidate. Uncle Wallace tells us of one Victory dance he remembers: it was broken up as soon as the first window was opened to cool off the hall. The defeated side thought it would be fun to toss a fresh-killed skunk into the room! For months after, as you can imagine, the perfume lingered on. Uncle Wallace says that he doesn't remember who was running for what in that election; but he'll never forget how it smelled!

Red pepper scattered over the floor and benches was a stunt which never failed to bring down the house in one universal sneeze. Liquor flowed freely, but for the most part it added zest rather than trouble. Trouble-makers, you see, were cordially bounced via the nape of the neck, by the floor managers. Musicians who loved the bottle were encouraged rather than squelched. We've heard tales about old Osgood, for instance, who, when high, could play melodies and variations in hoarse and speedy tones on the bass viol! At such times the remaining part of the orchestra, two fiddles, a cornet and a clarinet, always maintained an awed silence before this bull-frog phenomenon.

Chester Townes was another public tippler, but it was at last discovered that the quart of amber liquid he poured down his throat before taking up his violin, was nothing more noxious than cold tea. One drink of hard liquor would have knocked him out, but the substitute whet his whistle and served to create an envious reputation around town.

It wasn't the men who were solely responsible for shattering dance hall decorum. While most of the women were mouse-brown in their behavior in public, there were some like Edith Cram, who talked back many a time to a chiding prompter. This is something that must be done with a smile to be acceptable, and even then, you must make it an unusually personable smile. When, one time, she and her partner were lagging a bit behind, the caller shouted down in exactly the eight measures of the figure, "Come on, Edith, you are too slow." Edith, quick at metric repartee, chanted back, "We may be slow, Wallace, but by God, we're faithful."

So, these few scraps of background may give you an idea of our heritage, which makes it natural that we should still be enjoying the country dances throughout New England today.

Too much cannot be said for the summer and winter sportsters, New England's step- and grand-children. Ever since we have opened up our "guest chambers" to vacationers, or sold our farms to the neo-residents, the country dance picture has grown more and more encouraging.

At first, of course, the city folks didn't mix in. You couldn't blame them. Heaven knows, there's nothing more bewildering than a mess of high-stepping country dancers trying to follow a caller who's faster than a cat lapping up chain lightning! The visitors sat by, smiled, and occasionally were awed. Some bold ones tried the more simple figures but found that there was all the difference in the world between a Portland Fancy of today and what they thought they knew as a Portland Fancy in the days of their dancing school youth. And as for foxtrots, no amount of skill doing those would help in a country dance. And the "natives" didn't come to the rescue . . . not at first, that is. A combination of shyness and skepticism kept them back. But as soon as they realized that most city folks really wanted to learn the dances in a "serious" way, and that these people were not much different, after all, from themselves, then they opened up like umbrellas and were very generous in giving instruction.

The skiers were slightly harder to cope with, as a crowd. They were apt to be so keyed up, so out for a concentrated good weekend, so rash after their wild escapades on the snowy hills, and so free with their hard-toed ski boots (yes, they wear them at the dances—they're fine to shake 'er down in, if controlled), that we often feared for the results of the "mixed" crowd. But it all turned out just swell.

They're really a good bunch, with unusual vigor and a high I.Q., and with a little instruction they merged right in. And now, thanks to them, the winter country dances will surely survive. Before skiers, there had been some question in many towns whether the dances could be continued throughout the year.

Just as the skiers have changed the fate of winter country dances, so the dances have had their effect on skiing. When there's no snow, or when the conditions are poor (witness the winter of 1936-37), skiers can still hope for exercise and fun on their weekend dates in the country.

So, we say Country Dances, Ski Heil!

Now there is probably more to all of this than meets the eye. Modern country dancing has been responsible for a friendship of town and country, young and old, beginner and veteran, "high" and "low"— your husband dances with the maid, your daughter with a Polish mill hand and you may be teamed up with the oldest inhabitant, and all of you may be in the same set together. It's a workable democracy, a rare find in these democratic days.

And if you want to carry it further, you might even call it a pretty good design for living, too. How often we've thought of this in a Utopian light and wished we were a couple of big guys with bushy eyebrows and a Message for the Age. Then we could go out and preach about it. As it is, sometimes we almost get sufficiently inspired when we go to a country dance. If we ever do bubble over, we're going to hunt up a soap box and this is what we'll present with gestures.

THE COUNTRY DANCE PHILOSOPHY

Our first concern is with *The Spirit of the Whole* carried out by active co-operation. Everybody is both a doer and an observer, working out a pattern agreeable to all.

Next comes *Individualism*. Individualism of the ideal kind is encouraged: all, the dancers, the orchestra, the caller, may express themselves, improvise on the theme to their hearts' content, provided they show respect for the theme itself. (This brand of individualism differs from the pioneer kind, as it should, of course, in an age when frontiers are no longer open).

Pliability underlies this philosophy. By amendments each generation may accommodate the principles to its own needs.

Feeling for the Past and a *Forward-look* combine to remind us that the present and the future are but links in the same long chain.

Robustness, rather than degeneration (the mature child rather than the "sophisticated" adult), quite naturally results, since enjoyment springs from activity.

And activity encourages *Democracy* in the true sense . . . more so than the movies or the radio, which are only passively enjoyed by all.

Skill and *Control* are called forth in precision of timing the calls so that every step, plain or fancy, fits the basic beat of the music.

Everybody is kept busy. *Employment* is the rule, and the employment is fairly divided. However, "working hours" are short and intense, and leisure is not forgotten.

The *Good Neighbor Policy* flourishes. The country dance is the ideal foreign relationship. Here Poles, Finns, Canucks, Swedes, Yanks, Irish, Greeks, mix, and enjoy a common folk alliance.

There is *Freedom* in the real sense, as true freedom is working or playing together in harmony, not irresponsibility.

That, now, is what the country dance can mean. So we hereby nominate the Country Dance Plan as the first crocus in the recovery of civilization from its self-poisoning.

Any takers?

1976 note: Today we would be a little more formal about the nomenclature for these ethnic groups—French Canadian for *Canucks,* for instance.

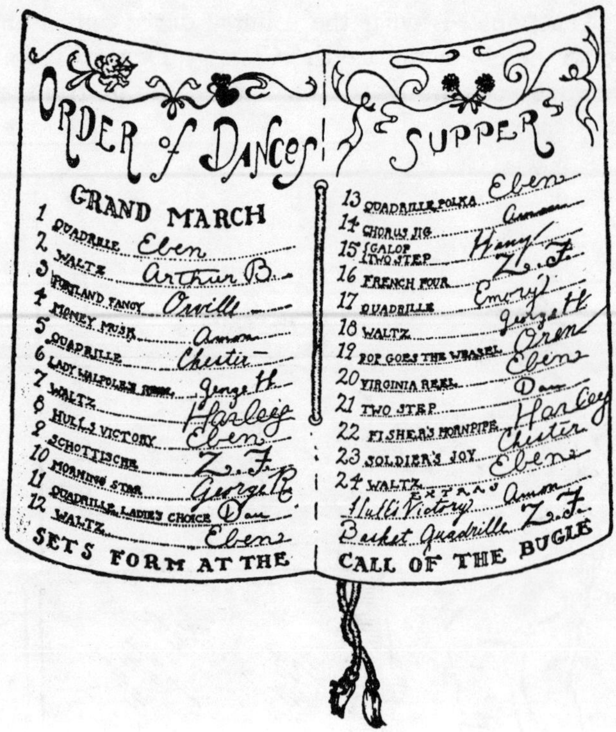

THE CALLS AND CONDUCT

A GENERAL GUIDE & GLOSSARY

OF TECHNIQUE & TERMS

Chapter II

IT MAKES good sense that the more off-stage dancing information you have at your command, the more fun and freedom you'll have when you come to dance. So we offer you some notes on general country dance technique, and list for your study a glossary of the terms that you'll need to know. And at the end of the chapter you will see rules for "making manners," a phrase dear to the hearts of all old-time dancing masters.

The first thing to remember is that the general style of country dancing is quite different from the style of any modern dance. While there is a slinking motion to the moderns, a sort of vertical motion characterizes the country dances. *Vertical* may be too strong a word; *liltingly buoyant* may be too long-haired poetical . . . but visualize something between the two as the ideal. Unless you are an expert at doing numerous little filligree steps and knee-toe brandishings, you had best stick to an easy, natural walking step for a while. You men, though, especially those of you who wish you were Fred Astaire, might adopt a little swagger . . . the merest suggestion of raising the elbows at each step and sometimes "scuffling" the feet. This always goes down big.

The next important thing to remember is to keep exact time to the music. Always wait until the prompter calls the figure before you begin it; or, if he doesn't actually call it, wait until the music suggests the next figure by a new phrase. And if your sense of rhythm isn't up to par and you finish a bit ahead of the others, wait in your place until the prompter and the music indicate your next change. This is important, not only for traffic reasons, but also for the appearance of the set. You *will* have your critics, you know, all too willing to rave about the way they stepped 'em out in their day.

After grace in style and good timing, individuality may then follow. In other words, first learn your fundamentals, and then you can try your "fancy Dan" steps. Gradually you will find yourself tapping to the beat while you wait your turn to dance, or maybe faking a sort of Charleston step of your own invention to garnish the unemployed moments. There is nothing like the realization of your own style to make you feel like the biggest pumpkin in the row.

As many people have found, the best way to learn the *changes* is to invite a good dancer to demonstrate them for you; and a wise plan is to throw a little junket of your own, inviting six or eight experienced couples. With study beforehand, you ought to make progress this way—and we mean *real* study. Don't be satisfied with a smattering of knowledge. As in everything else, a little knowledge is a dangerous thing; better to have no dancing information than to be content with knowing just a little about all the changes. So read and re-read this chapter, even if you don't crack the rest of the book.

Best practice one figure until it comes to you as naturally as breathing. The way to master any call is to stick with it until you have it down cold; then pass on to another. Next, combine the two into a phrase, and then make a sentence with a few phrases. Whew! There'll be no stopping you then. Since you have little chance today of finding a dancing master nearby to make you keep in practice, it is all up to you—like not cheating at Solitaire. Perhaps in a few more years dancing schools will be re-established, for we have heard rumors of there being two or three started already.

Usually the music is divided into measures of eight, and less often into fours and sixteens. These are the music bars, and the counts required to carry out the figures are two counts, or steps, to each bar. It doesn't take long to get used to feeling through the music and sensing the counts. To help you do

1976 note: Country dance instruction is indeed on the **wax, as a look** at the backmatter will show.

this, the bars of music are indicated throughout. Remember that each bar requires two steps. That is, "Right and left (4)" means that there are four bars of music to which you do eight steps.

In a quadrille, or any of the dances where four couples form a square, the least experienced ones should take their places at the sides, rather than at the head or foot. This is because the head and foot couples do the changes first. The sides do a carbon-copy of them and so have a chance to stand by and see the figures demonstrated before their turn comes. The head couple are the ones with their backs to the music; the foot couple face the music.

In a contry dance, where two parallel lines face "contrary" to each other, beginners should avoid the key positions which are generally the first, third, fifth, etc., couples. In some dances the first and fourth begin. Watch out for this: at the bottom of all the dance recipes in this book you will see which couples begin the figures. The couples indicated, then, start the dance, while the others wait and repeat the figure when they get to the head of the line. The prompter always announces which couples begin in both a contry and quadrille, so you really don't have to worry. For instance, he might say for a quadrille: "First four, right and left." That means the head and foot couples only; the side couples just watch during this call. And in a contry, he might announce: "First, third and fifth couples down the outside and back"; or the same announcement in another way,

"Head and every other couple down the outside and back." That is, the couple nearest the music and every other couple down the line begin. The other couples stand by until the head is reached. There are usually six or eight couples in a contry set, although there are sometimes more. The design of the hall has much to do with the arrangement and size of the sets.

❧

GLOSSARY

The terms given here are the ones you'll hear most often in the dances of New England, at least. Most of them are the fundamental calls of country dancing, square or contry variety, and once you've mastered them all, you'll have no cause for worry. When the prompter roars, "Gents bow, the ladies know how," the call will be as familiar to you as the palm of your hand. When he calls, "Turn your opposite twice around, kick her in the shins and knock her down," you can be smug as anything as you realize that this is only a call in Hull's Victory, dressed up to kill. You'll know that "Ladies Chain" is "Ladies Chain" whether it occurs in a quadrille or a Morning Star, and your studies will have told you that "Swing your partner" is identical with "Turn your partner."

With the help of the illustrations, we think you'll have little or no trouble in understanding the calls.

PARTNERS: In a quadrille, the lady, when in place, stands to the right of the gent. In a contry, partners stand opposite each other in line.

CORNERS: This is a position found only in the square formation. A gent's corner is the lady on his left; likewise, a lady's corner is the gent on her right.

ADDRESS PARTNERS: (8 bars) Used in quadrilles. The gent steps forward to center with left foot, turns and faces partner; closes right foot to left and bows. At the same time, the lady slides right foot to center, faces partner, steps back with left foot, bending both knees for the curtsey, then draws left foot to right.

ADDRESS CORNERS: (8 bars) Gent bows to lady on his left, while his partner bows to gent on her right.

ALLEMANDE RIGHT: (8) Lady walks 4 steps to left, passing in front of her partner. Gent walks 4 steps to right. Each meets new partner on corner, they join right hands and turn once around, walk back to place and balance partner.

ALLEMANDE LEFT

ALLEMANDE LEFT (8) Couples turn back to back and walk 4 steps to meet their corner, thus each meeting new partner; these join left hands and turn once around, return to place (4 steps) and balance partner.

BALANCE CORNERS: (4) Used only in quadrille. The same steps as in balance partners but they are executed with your corner.

BALANCE PARTNERS: (4) Partners face each other, then each step to the side with right foot, point toe of left foot in front, step back to place with left and point toe of right foot in front of left foot.

BALANCE AND SWING PARTNER: (8) Originally the balance step was performed before the swing, but nowadays this has been almost universally abandoned, and the call now means only to swing, or turn, your partner. (This probably accounts for the lack of enthusiasm over dances having lots of balance steps and little swinging. Modern youth is really swing crazy in more ways than one. Especially is this true throughout most of Massachusetts. There they swing when there's little necessity for doing so. In Hull's Victory, where the second command is given "turn with left hand twice around," a call which is generally obeyed by joining left arms at the elbow with the opposite and reeling twice around, in Massachusetts a regular "swing partner" position is taken with the opposite, and partners spin about two or three times in that manner.)

CHASSEZ RIGHT OR LEFT: (4) A gliding step is used with either foot in the direction desired. If to the left, the left foot glides and the right is drawn to it and repeated as often as desired.

CAST OFF: (4) Means to go below one couple and is done usually after "down the center and back," like this: Gent will place his left arm about the next gent's waist, and in that position both turn once around to the left, stopping so that the one who casts off is below one place. At the same time, the lady places her right arm about the waist of the next lady, and in that position both turn once around to the right, stopping so that the lady who cast off is below one place. (In Massachusetts this is an excuse to swing vigorously. In certain parts of New Hampshire, cast off is done by the couples separating, going across the set and standing to the left of the person they have cast off.)

ALL PROMENADE: (8) In a quadrille this means that the couples march around the set side by side, in the direction opposite to the hands of a clock. Most contry dances are brought to a finish by the call "All promenade around the hall."

CROSS RIGHT HANDS HALF AROUND: (4) Four ladies or gents, as the prompter may direct, give right hands to the opposite, walk in a half circle to the left and then stop.

LEFT HANDS BACK: (4) From above position they turn, cross left hands with the opposite and walk back to place.

DOS A DOS (BACK TO BACK): (4) Lady and gent forward, pass to left of each other; that is, right shoulder to right shoulder; having gone one step past each other, take one step to the right, which brings the couple back to back. Without turning, back around each other and walk backward to place.

DOWN THE CENTER AND BACK: (8) This call occurs in contry dances. In ordinary position side by side, the couples walk down the hall between the two lines of dancers who are waiting their turn. They take eight steps down the center, then face about and walk eight steps back.

DOWN THE CENTER

DOWN THE OUTSIDE AND BACK: (8) This also is a contry dance call. The gent and lady go eight steps down the outside of their respective sets, behind the inactive lines of couples. They then face about and retrace their steps back to place.

EIGHT HANDS AROUND: (8) Used in a quadrille, or square. The eight dancers making up the set join hands and circle once around to the left. Four and six hands around are done in the same manner, the only difference being the number of dancers involved.

FORWARD AND BACK: (4) Start with the left foot and advance 3 steps. On the 4th count bring right foot raised to the heel of the left foot. Now, starting with right foot walk backwards 3 steps to place, and on the 4th count, bring left foot up in front.

FORWARD, AND LADIES TO CENTER: (8) All join hands and forward 3 steps as before, then back to place as before, then forward again 3 steps; the ladies drop their partners' hands and stand in center together; gents walk back to place.

FORM A BASKET: (8) With ladies in the center as above, facing each other, the men walk forward, so as to stand at the left hand of their partners. Gents now join hands, the ladies bow slightly forward, allowing the men to raise their joined hands over the ladies' heads. The ladies now step back one step and join hands.

GRAND RIGHT AND LEFT: (16) Face partners, join right hands, gents moving to the right and the ladies to the left. Gents now drop partners' hand and take the next lady's left hand in his left; next with the right, and so on around the set back to place. (This is a movement in which the two lines, moving in opposite directions, weave in and out.) When half around, each gent will meet his partner giving her his right hand; both make slight bow to each other, then continue to place.

GRAND ALLEMANDE: (32) Each gent links right arm with partner and turns once around, then gives left arm to the next lady and turns her once around, right to the next, and so on around the set to place. The movement is similar to grand right and left, the gents moving to the right and the ladies to the left.

HALF PROMENADE: (4) The couples join hands and chassez across the set to the opposite side, where they turn half-round to the left, facing in opposite direction. They are now ready for:

HALF RIGHT AND LEFT: (4) The couples cross back to place, the ladies on the inside so that, in passing, the gents are on the ladies' right.

LADIES CHAIN: (8) Ladies cross to the opposite's place, giving right hands as they pass each other, and their left hands to the opposite gent who turns them once around. They give right hand back, left hand to partners who turn them once around to the left. In turning, the gents join left hands with the ladies, and place their right hand about the lady's waist. (In Massachusetts, Ladies Chain is done this way: instead of turning partner in open position as above described, the couples take a waltz position, each lady swinging in this fashion two or three times around with the opposite gent and then with her partner.)

LADIES GRAND CHAIN: (8) Same as Ladies Chain except all four ladies are involved. This call is used only in quadrilles.

GENTS GRAND CHAIN: (8) Same as preceding call, only gents chain instead of the ladies.

PROMENADE FOUR: (8) Gent takes his partner's left hand in his left, places his right arm about her waist and advances toward the opposite couple who are coming to meet them; they pass to right of each other and take each other's places. Turn half around and return to place in same manner.

RIGHT AND LEFT: (8) Two opposite couples cross over, ladies on the inside. When in the opposite couple's place, the gents take their partners' left hand in their left and both turn half around. Repeat to place.

TURN PARTNERS: (4) Also called *SWING PARTNERS*. This is the most difficult step of them all to learn, and considerable practice is needed before you can become adept. It really is a sort of pivot step. The gent holds the lady he is swinging in a waltz position, but well out to the right, so that they are nearly side by side, right shoulder to right shoulder. In this position, move quickly to the right like this: On "one," put down the right foot in place, on "and," step forward with the left foot. On "two" put down the right foot on the same spot as before, on "and" step forward with the left foot again, and so on. You are really using the right foot as a pivotal base, and the left foot as a paddle to turn you in a circle; hence, more weight should be put on the right foot than on the left. You should practice this so that you can enjoy the figure to the fullest, for it is unanimously considered the best call ever invented.

SWING CONTRY CORNERS: This call is found only in Chorus Jig and is done after casting off. The active couples advance to the center of the set, passing to the right of each other. The lady turns the gent standing at the head of the set with her left hand, while her partner turns the third lady with his left hand. The same couple advance to center of the set again passing to the right of each other as before. The lady turns the third gent with her left hand while her partner turns the lady standing at the head of the set with his left hand. This leaves the gent standing between two ladies, and his partner standing between two gents, ready for the next call.

❧

CONDUCT

Now, in considering making manners on the dance floor, the underlying rules for making manners anywhere else apply: common sense and a social feeling. There is nothing difficult, new or mysterious about the do's and don'ts of the country dance.

The idea, as we've pointed out, is the spirit of the whole. So, prancing, jumping, dancing stiff-legged, stamping, and flinging your arms about like a mad wind-mill, are taboo for obvious reasons. On the other hand, being relaxed and carefree is extremely acceptable.

To be relaxed and have the most fun you must consider your clothes. Stiff collar and tie, vest and coat, are, of course, not the things to wear at a real country dance. Remember that country dancing is no sissy stuff and that you reach the boiling point early in the evening—a condition which a muggy summer night or a white-hot stove do not enhance. If you are a "gent," come prepared to strip down to open-necked shirt, and if you are a lady (or even a woman), a cotton or silk gathered or circular skirt is the thing.

In the old days the picture was quite the reverse. One had to be "hail fellow, well met," in the difficult clothes of the day, or just not come. It was considered the height of impropriety to unbutton a collar or loosen a tie in public, and as for taking the coat completely off and rolling up your sleeves—heavens! that was as bad as eating with your knife with all the shades pulled up. If some bold gent did attempt to break the rules, the floor managers couldn't get to him quickly enough to tell him . . . not to ask him . . . to dress up or get out. Even if he escaped notice, no lady would have accepted his invitation to dance!

In the matter of introductions the picture has also changed. Long ago the floor managers saw to it that strangers were introduced and that no dancing went on without benefit of formal approach. Today, at a public dance, as long as a stranger is sober and otherwise decent in his behavior, no gal need refuse him a dance. And if she knows the dances and swings in a lusty fashion, she need have no fear of being a wall-flower. It makes no difference in a country dance whether your partner is young or old, married or single, slim or fat, pretty or homely . . . if she or he can step it out to the beat, that is all that matters.

To be sure, you don't always get the partner of your dreams, but a country dance is less cruel than a modern slinkabout in that, by constant interchanging, it safeguards you from being hooked with the same person all evening.

Some of the rules which the dancing masters used to expound when gramma was a girl are still perennials. Here is a list of them * as taught by Lucien O. Carpenter, "Philadelphia's Leading Dancing Master."

1. A lady or gentleman should finish their toilet before entering the room for dancing, as it is indecorous in either to be drawing on their gloves, or brushing their hair. Finish your toilet in the dressing rooms.

2. A lady should have an easy, becoming and graceful movement while engaged in a quadrille or promenade. It is more pleasing to the gentleman.

3. A gentleman should make himself sociable, easy and agreeable in dancing.

* From J. W. Pepper's *Prompter's Call-Book and Violinist's Guide.*

4. A lady should never engage herself for more than the following set, unless by the consent of the gentleman who accompanies her.

5. It is very impolite and insulting in either lady or gentleman while dancing in a quadrille, to mar the pleasure of others by galloping around or inside of the next set.

6. A gentleman who conducts a lady to a quadrille, should remain until finished, and not leave it to go into another set, as it is an insult to those you have left.

7. It is very indecorous, and out of place, to give way to immoderate laughing, sneering or commenting at those who are present. It certainly shows a want of refinement.

8. Recollect, the desire of imparting pleasure, especially to the ladies, is one of the essential qualifications of a gentleman.

9. A gentleman during a quadrille and when in society, should, in his salutations, make a slight bow, bending the body forward with ease and dignity; avoid bowing too low.

10. It is the duty of a gentleman having a place in a quadrille to have his lady with him, otherwise he forfeits his place.

11. Never take part in a quadrille without knowing something of the figures; lead your lady, gently taking her fingers, and not grasp her hand.

12. The customary honors of a bow and courtesy are given at the commencement of every dance, likewise at its conclusion, when the gentleman will conduct his partner to her seat, bow and retire, unless he chooses to sit beside her.

13. At the supper hour the gentleman conducts to the supper-room the lady whom he escorts, and will remain with her while at table, seeing that all her wants are attended to.

Mr. Carpenter speaks only of quadrilles; doubtless the quadrille was used to symbolize all the dances. Anyway, the same rules apply to them all.

And here are some of Mr. Carpenter's less applicable rules which will probably strike you as funny as they did us. First, he started with a series of *emilyposts* for street behavior, to get you in a decorous mood for the dance, no doubt. "1. The lady should be the first to recognize an acquaintance, whether intimate or not," says Mr. Carpenter.

2. The gentleman should raise his hat slightly, inclining and turning toward the lady in saluting. The hat should be raised by the hand furthest from the lady.

3. One salutation is all that civility requires when passing a person more than once on a public promenade or drive.

4. The gentleman should raise his hat when asking a lady's pardon for an inadvertence, whether she is known to him or not.

5. Never stare at any one, is a rule with no exceptions.

6. The gentleman should not smoke when driving or walking with ladies.

7. Should you desire to converse with a lady you should happen to meet, do not detain her, but turn and walk in her direction.

8. Loud conversation should be avoided at all times.

And etiquette for the ballroom:

1. If a gentleman wishes to dance with a lady with whom he is not acquainted, respectfully ask the director for an introduction.

2. Ladies should not be too hasty in filling their programme on their entrance to the ballroom, as they may have cause to regret should a friend happen to enter.

3. An introduction in a public ballroom must be understood by the gentleman to be for that evening only, after which the acquaintanceship ceases, unless the lady chooses to recognize it at any future time or place.

4. It is not correct to ask a married lady to dance, her husband being present, without having first ascertained whether it is agreeable to him.

5. Gloves should be removed at the supper table.

On one side of the fireplace in the assembly room in Mr. Whidden's Portsmouth Tavern this set of rules greeted all dancers:

NO STRANGER ADMISSIBLE WITHOUT A TICKET, SIGNED BY ONE OF THE MANAGERS, AND PREVIOUSLY OBTAINED.

NO GENTLEMAN ADMISSIBLE IN BOOTS, COLORED STOCKINGS OR UNDRESS.

Another item admonishes: "Go to a public ball about eight o'clock. To a private ball the time of going depends on the invitation. The hour should be adhered to as nearly as possible, as those who are punctual feel uncomfortable until the other guests arrive. Besides, it looks as if you wished to appear of great importance, when you make your entrance at a late hour."

We wish we had room to reprint more of the old rules, but, after all, we must get "on with the dance."

THE DANCE
BEGINS

GRAND MARCHES & SICILIAN CIRCLE

Chapter III

SINCE there probably never was a formal dance in the old days that didn't start off with a Grand March and Circle, we're going to initiate you with these simplest of dances. Merely warm-up numbers, they naturaly were used only to introduce the more strenuous dances on the program.

To describe *the* way to do a Grand March would be much like trying to tell you *the* way to make hash. In fact, a Grand March is quite like a good hash . . . a little of this and a little of that, and zip, what is it?

Any Grand March needs to be led off by a person of experience and imagination, with a good sense of ceremony to boot. All marching should be done in straight lines following the directions of the walls; the change of direction is made precisely at each corner. Gents will offer their right arms to partners and move slowly about the room once or twice, giving all couples time to fall in and follow.

THE MARCH IN FILE

When all are placed in order the leader heads the line of march up the room; reaching the top, he turns to the left and his partner to the right. The gents follow him in single file, and the ladies follow his partner in the same manner. When the leaders reach the bottom of the room they pass to the left of each other, the gents marching round the room on the outside and the ladies on the inside and in opposite directions. When the first gent meets his partner again at the top of the room they both march together around the room to the right followed by the other couples. The leader must continue the plain marching between each figure long enough to get all the couples following him before commencing a new change.

THE MARCH IN THE COLUMN

The first couple lead round the room until the leader reaches the bottom left hand corner. There, instead of turning at right angles up the side of the room, the first couple should file to the right and march in a line parallel with the advancing couples, but in an opposite direction across the room; as each couple successively arrives at the same corner, they file to the right and follow their leader. When the leader has got across the room, the first couple should file to the left, and march straight across the room and back again, and so on, forming a serpentine line of march backwards and forwards across the room until the head of the hall is reached. They then lead around the room again until all the couples are following in regular column.

THE ARBOR MARCH

All the couples march around the room in order. The first couple join right hands at the head of the room, stop and raise their hands, thus forming an arch. The second couple pass underneath the arch, the gent first, and form another arch; the third couple pass under both, and also form an arch, and so on, each couple passing through the arches ahead of them in turn, until one continuous arch has been formed. The first couple then passes through and out at the end of the arbor, followed by each couple in succession until the arches have all disappeared. The first couple can follow the last couple at once under the arches if desired and repeat the arbor continuously as long as desired. The plain march by couples is then resumed until the couples are in regular formation again.

THE PLATOON

First couple lead march up center of the room. Arriving there the first couple passes round to the right, second couple to the left, the remaining odd couples in their order to the right and the even couples following to the left. All thus march down their side of the room until they meet at the bottom; there they turn up the center again four abreast. Upon reaching the top, the first four wheel round to the right, the second four, to the left and so on alternately, each division marching down their side of the hall. Upon meeting at the bottom, they advance up the center eight abreast. The same procedure as before is followed and up the center sixteen abreast, thus forming full lines. At the top of the room all halt, the first, third, etc., lines all face to the right, the second, fourth, etc., lines all face to the left. Then gentlemen step up beside their partners and the front line marches off in couples to the right, the other lines following in the same manner as in the march by columns.

Eventually, the first couple will lead the march around the hall once or twice, then will signal the leader of the orchestra and the music will stop. As soon as this occurs the first, third, fifth, etc., couples will turn around to their right and face the following couple. This is the proper position for the Sicilian Circle. The music changes, and the dance is on.

SICILIAN CIRCLE

Four hands twice around	8 bars
Both couples join hands in circle and move rapidly to the left.	
Right and left	8 "
Ladies chain	8 "
Forward and back	4 "
Forward again and pass on to the next	4 "

In Connecticut this dance is known as the Single Reel, but more widely it is known as the Portland Fancy. Just where or when it acquired this name nobody knows. Surely it bears little resemblance to the original Portland Fancy. Time has proved it a very popular dance, and it is often played twice or more times in an evening. Every fiddler or orchestra leader has his own idea of what is the best tune to play for the dance. Most of them agree on one point: that no matter what tune they start with, after playing it two or three times, they shift to some other piece written in the same key, and after giving that a good going over, they shift again to yet another tune, so that when the dance is ended they may have played a half dozen or more jigs, varying in number with the ability of the musicians. The dance lends itself to such a variety of tunes. It usually begins at a very moderate speed, but the frequent changing of tunes seems to work the fiddlers into a frenzy and they play faster and faster, until the end finds them perspiring nearly as much as the dancers.

In some parts of New England you may find the Circle done as follows:

All forward and back	4	bars
Four hands around	4	"
Ladies chain	8	"
Right and left	4	"
All balance partners	4	"
Promenade once and a half around	8	"

Repeat figures as long as desired.

The last call is done like this:

Gentlemen take partner's left hand in their left, place right arm about the lady's waist and promenade once and a half around and finish facing the next new couple.

For variety some prompters add a bit of Soldier's Joy into the Circle. On such occasions the dance will usually end with everybody joining hands in one big circle around the hall. The prompter then calls, "Grand right and left." When all have progressed about half way round the room he calls "All turn partners and promenade the hall." The confusion resulting from this "seek-wife-in-the-dark" business, never fails to put every one in good humor for what is to follow.

THE SUCCOTASH QUADRILLE

HATS OFF TO FRANCE

SOME QUADRILLES & OTHER SQUARES

Chapter IV

First, we're going to start right off and disillusion you (in a nice way, of course) . . . that is, if you are one of those who insist on calling all old-fashioned dances, *square dances*. Maybe you know better, but have just fallen into a misnaming habit, same's we all get into. But since habits like this are apt to stick like poor cousins if we don't do anything about them, let's get it clear once and for all: *Square dance* refers, strictly speaking, *only* to those dances done in square formation. Logical enough, isn't it? Of these, the most numerous are the quadrilles. But there are lots of non-quadrilles that are also square dances. Few of

---

Note.—The manuscript from which this music was taken has been in the possession of the Page family for over fifty years. It was a favorite of Sewall Page.

these non-quadrille squares rate very high in this corner of the country, though. The ones that are still danced will be described later in this chapter. But now for the quadrille.

The quadrille, more or less as we do it now, was hatched in the French court ballet. It so fascinated everybody that it immediately took hold and spread like measles in a kindergarten. It whisked across the channel, and after getting well established in the British Isles, it found its way to America. To this day it is in great demand; if anything, it is more of a pet than ever.

As you would suppose from its name, this is a *drill* with couples in *quad*rangular formation. Four couples make up a set, each forming one side of a perfect square. (Remember that the head couple always have their backs to the music and the foot couple face the music; and that the head and foot couples begin the dance. Also remember that the lady stands to the right of the gent when in place.) The size of the hall is the only limit to the number of sets that can dance at one time.

Quadrilles were originally divided into five sections, each with its appropriate music and four brief intermissions, just long enough to catch the breath and flirt a bit. In recent years they have been shortened to three sections to suit the less leisurely times, with two intermissions, doubtless for the original purpose.

It is impossible to speculate on how many quadrilles there have been, for the actual number of recorded ones, alone, would stagger an adding machine. When you consider that every program included from six to a dozen of these five-figured dances fifty years ago, you can imagine how many quadrilles must have been concocted. And when you also consider that the topnotch prompters could call that many dances without repeating a single command, you can see why they were called "the good old days."

The basic quadrille is the so-called Plain Quadrille (why was it ever called *plain?*), and from that developed variations. There was the Lancers, the Basket, the Caledonian, the Harlequin, the Social, the Hibernian, and the Cheat or Ninepin, to name only a few of the most favored. With the arrival of countless round dances, the Waltz, the Polka, the Mazourka, the Redowa, the Galop, the Schottische, and the Polka-Redowa Quadrilles came into being. All these last named were novelty dances, and as soon as the shine wore off, they were promptly discarded, so that today they are but memories. There was some beautiful music written for the Waltz Quadrilles, and the figures were graceful and not too difficult. Just why they fell from grace is one of the mysteries of the dance world.

Rather than give you the orthodox quadrilles or the novelty variations (which, after all, you can find elsewhere), we are presenting at the end of this chapter, some more or less original quadrilles of the "plain" variety. Many of these figures are those called by contemporary New England prompters and have never before seen print. We think you'll enjoy them.

You will notice that there are a parcel of French terms used in the quadrille. That is due to the influence of the early dancing masters in this country, most of them Frenchmen who came to the colonies to recoup personal fortunes squandered abroad. Many of them sailed over with the French troops during the Revolution, and seeing the possibilities of following their profession on these shores, they never sailed back. Quite a few joined traveling theatrical troupes that wandered up and down the Atlantic coast, giving lessons at every stop.

One of the most picturesque of these men was Chateaubriand. He claimed to have been cook for Rochambeau during the Revolution. One day, some years after Yorktown, he was found near the Vermont-New York boundary busily engaged in teaching a group of half-naked Iroquois the latest quadrille steps! For many years this Frenchman wandered about New England giving lessons in ballroom manners. His coach-and-four consisted of an old plug horse and heavy wagon; his pay, poultry, venison, bear meat and vegetables.

The various figures of all quadrilles are a combination of elementary movements, each with a name of its own. These movements must be thoroughly digested beforehand. because the prompter shouts only the name of the figure, having no time to enter into explanation with this or that couple on the floor. Much of the fun of quadrilles is the spirit of competition which exists between the prompter and you. He loves to give a surprise call in your most unguarded moments, though usually he is kind enough not to give any outlandish commands without first explaining them. Having some eighty-nine calls in his magic kit, you can see the reason for the quadrille's popularity.

When regular quadrille music is played, the first eight bars are merely preparatory, during which all salute. Each gent bows first to his partner, then to the lady on his left . . . his corner; each lady, at the same time, bows first to her partner, then to the gent on her right . . . her corner.

If the music happens to be made up of jigs, reels, old-time ballads, or modern pieces, the dancers join hands at once and execute a rapid eight hands around to the left, and an equally fast return to the right.

Each year more and more prompters and orchestras favor this latter type of music, because they feel that it has more pep than the music written solely for the quadrille. That, of course, is a matter of opinion, but it is certainly true that such music is far more adaptable for rhyming the changes as so many of the present prompters do. The use of this form of music for quadrilles is probably, as we pointed out in the beginning chapter, directly due to the old kitchen junkets.

Thanks to the radio with its barn dance bands, the rhyming caller is highly popular. Some dashing tunes for these "modern quadrilles" are: Darling Nellie Gray, Girl I Left Behind Me, Buffalo Gals, Steamboat Quickstep, Garry Owen, Kingdom Coming, Wearing of the Green, Coming Round the Mountain, Bonnie Dundee, and, would you believe it, Hinkey Dinkey Parley Voo. The field for pioneering is limitless, of course. Probably The Parade of the Wooden Soldiers, Valencia, Barcelona, Marching Along Together and dozens more will be tried and found to fit.

If you prefer the other type . . . the standard quadrille music . . . then you will find the following hard to beat: Sailor's Return, The Black Cat, Queen Bee, Circus, Prince of Good Fellows, Autumn Leaves and Harvest Moon.

The steps in a quadrille are much simpler than those used in the contrys. The feet should be raised only a very little from the floor, and the motions of the body should be easy and natural. You should lead your partner as gracefully as possible through the figures and not try to show off too much with pigeon's wings or High Betty Martins. Such decorations do well enough in a jig or hornpipe, but are as out of place in a quadrille as a jug of hard cider in the home of a W. C. T. U. leader.

Wait a minute! There go a few bars of the Black Cat. Here's a chance to find out how well you have mastered your ABC's.

PLAIN QUADRILLE # 1

Figure One

Wait eight bars, bow to partner, then to your corner.

First four, right and left	8	bars
Same four, ladies chain	8	"
Half right and left	4	"
Half promenade	4	"
All balance and turn partners	8	"
All promenade	8	"

Sides now repeat same figures.

Figure Two

First couple lead to right and four hands around	8	bars
Lead to next and right and left	8	"
Lead to the last and ladies chain	8	"
All forward and back, turn partners	8	"
All promenade	8	"

Other three couples do the figure in turn.

Figure Three

All join hands and circle eight hands around	8	bars
Four ladies grand chain	8	"
Grand right and left	16	"
Eight hands around	8	"
Four gents grand chain	8	"
Grand right and left	16	"
All forward and back, turn partners	8	"

All promenade to seats.

PLAIN QUADRILLE # 2

Figure One

Wait eight bars, bow to partner, then to your corner.

First four half right and left	4	bars
Promenade across and back	8	"
Half right and left to place	4	"
Same four ladies chain	8	"
Promenade	8	"
Ladies grand chain	8	"
Balance and turn partner	8	"

Sides now repeat same figures.

Figure Two

First four forward and back	4	bars
Forward again and four hands half around	4	"
First four ladies chain	8	"
Forward four	4	"
Half right and left to place	4	"
Grand right and left	16	"
All balance and turn partners	8	"

Sides now repeat same figures.

Figure Three

All join hands and circle eight hands around	8	bars
Four ladies grand chain	8	"
Grand right and left	16	"
Eight hands around	8	"
Four gentlemen grand chain	8	"
Grand right and left	16	"
All forward and back, turn partners	8	"

All promenade to seats.

PLAIN QUADRILLE # 3

Figure One

Wait first eight bars, addressing partner, then your corner.

First four half right and left	4	bars
Promenade	8	"
Half right and left to place	4	"
Same four ladies chain	8	"
Promenade	8	"
Ladies grand chain	8	"
Balance and turn partner	8	"

Sides now repeat same figures.

Figure Two

First four forward and back	4	bars
Forward again and four hands half around	4	"
First four ladies chain	8	"
Forward four	4	"
Half right and left to place	4	"
Grand right and left	16	"
All balance and turn partners	8	"

Sides now repeat same figures.

Figure Three

Eight hands around, to the left	8	bars
Other way back to place	8	"
Grand right and left	16	"
Four ladies forward and stand in center	4	"
Gents four hands around the outside	4	"
Form a basket	4	"
Eight hands around as you are	8	"
All turn partners	8	"
All forward and turn the opposite	8	"
All turn partners	8	"

Ladies grand chain	8	bars
All turn corners	8	"
Four gents forward and stand in center	4	"
Ladies four hands around the outside	4	"
Form a basket	4	"
Eight hands around as you are	8	"
All turn partners	8	"
Grand right and left	16	"
All forward and back	4	"
All turn partners	8	"

All promenade around the hall.

GRAND RIGHT AND LEFT

PLAIN QUADRILLE # 4

Figure One

Wait first eight bars, addressing partner, then your corner.

First four right and left	8	bars
Sides right and left	8	"
First four balance and turn partners	8	"
Sides balance and turn partners	8	"
First four ladies chain	8	"
Side four ladies chain	8	"
Four ladies grand chain	8	"
All promenade	8	"

Figure Two

First couple lead to the right	4	bars
Join hands and circle once around	4	"
Four lead to next, six hands around	8	"
Six lead to next, eight hands around	8	"
First four half promenade	4	"
Half right and left to place	4	"

Other couples repeat in turn.

Figure Three

All allemande left	4	bars
Grand right and left	16	"
Four ladies grand chain	8	"
All allemande left	4	"
Grand right and left	16	"
All forward and back, swing your partners	8	"

All promenade around the hall.

PLAIN QUADRILLE # 5

Figure One

Wait eight bars, address partners, then your corners.

Head lady and opposite gent forward and back, forward again and dos a dos	8	bars
Forward four and balance the opposite	4	"
Four hands half around	4	"
Head gent and opposite lady forward and back, forward again and dos a dos	8	"
Forward four and balance the opposite	4	"
Half right and left to place	4	"
Ladies grand chain	8	"

Other couples repeat in turn.

Figure Two

First four forward and back	4	bars
Turn the opposite	4	"
All balance partners, turn corners	8	"
Sides forward and back	4	"
Turn the opposite	4	"
All balance corners, turn partners	8	"
First four half promenade, half right and left	8	"
Sides half promenade, half right and left	8	"
All forward and back, turn partners	8	"
All promenade	8	"

Figure Three

All balance partners, turn corners	8	bars
Four ladies cross right hands, walk half round	4	"
Turn, give left hand back, right hand to partner	4	"
All balance and turn partners	8	"
Grand right and left	16	"

Four gents cross right hands, half around	4 bars
Left hand back, give right hand to partner	4 "
All balance and turn partners	8 "
Allemande left	4 "
Grand right and left	16 "

All forward and back, promenade to seats.

PLAIN QUADRILLE # 6

Figure One

Wait eight bars, addressing partners, then your corners.

First four lead to right, right and left with that couple	8 bars
Promenade the same	8 "
Ladies chain, the same	8 "
Promenade the same	8 "

The side couples now lead to the right and repeat the changes, ending with all promenade around the set.

Figure Two

First four lead to the right, cross right hands half way round	4 bars
Left hand back	4 "
All balance partners	4 "
All half promenade	4 "
Ladies forward and back	4 "
Gents forward and back	4 "
Half right and left to place	4 "

The side couples now lead to the right and repeat the changes, ending with grand right and left.

Figure Three

Grand right and left	16	bars
Head couple promenade inside of set and face out	4	"
Other couples form in line	4	"
All chassez to center of hall and back to place	8	"
March, ladies to right and gents to left	8	"
All forward and back, turn partners	8	"

Other couples repeat in turn, ending with all
promenade to seats.

PLAIN QUADRILLE # 7

As called by Happy Hale, of Bernardston, Mass.

Figure One

MUSIC: Turkey in the Straw

Join your hands and once around
The other way back, you're going wrong
Swing your partners everyone
And all promenade
Head gent turn right hand lady with right hand around
Left hand lady with left hand around
Opposite lady with both hands around
Turn partner in center, and six hands around

Other gents repeat changes in turn.

Figure Two

MUSIC: Devil's Dream

Eight hands once around and back the other way
First lady lead to right, swing that gent and hug him tight
Lead to next and on your toes, swing that man with the big
red nose

Swing the next one standing there, run your fingers through
his hair
Now lead to the last and swing your own, everybody swing
You swing yours and I'll swing mine. I'd rather swing yours
most any time
All promenade. Put your arms around her waist and promenade
right to your place

Other ladies repeat the changes in turn.

Figure Three

MUSIC: Darling Nellie Gray

Eight hands around
The first head couple lead up to the right, join your hands and
circle once around
Now you right and left right through and you right and left
right back
And you swing your darling Nellie Gray
Lead to the next, and you balance all around
Join your hands and circle once around
Now you right and left right through and you right and left
right back
And you swing your darling Nellie Gray
Lead to the last and you balance all around
Join your hands and circle once around
Now you right and left right through and you right and left
right back
And you all swing your darling Nellie Gray
Allemande left with the lady on your left
And grand right and left half around
When you meet your partner, on the other side
You promenade with your darling Nellie Gray

Other couples repeat in turn.

PLAIN QUADRILLE # 8

As called by Ambrose LaNue, of Charlemont, Mass.

Figure One

MUSIC: French Jig

Eight hands around and back the other way
First couple lead to right and balance that couple
The lady walk around the lady and the gent around the gent
The lady round the gent and the gent around the lady
Four hands half around
Swing partner

      Repeat the same changes with other two couples.

Then dos ? dos your corner all,
And do the same with your own little doll
Right hand to your partners all and right and left around the hall

Figure Two

MUSIC: Garry Owen

Join your hands and once around, everybody once around
With your right foot up and your left foot down
Hurry up Joe you'll never get around
The other way back you are going wrong
Balance to your corners all, swing that girl around the hall
Leave her alone and swing your own, everybody swing your own
The first couple lead to the right
Circle four with all your might
Lead to the next and don't get mixed
Cross your right hands half way round
Pay attention to what I say, give left hands back the other way
Now lead to the last and ladies chain
The other two ladies do the same
Join your hands and forward all, swing that gal across the hall
Now run away home and swing your own

Right hand to your partners all, right and left around the hall
When you meet her pass her by
Kiss the next one on the sly
Poke the next one in the eye
Swing your own girl by and by
Swing her once, swing her twice
Swing her again if she is not your wife

Figure Three

MUSIC: *Little Brown Jug*

First couple promenade round the outside of the set
Swing partner
First couple down the center and cast off six
Lady go right and gent go left
Swing partner
Same couple down the center, cast off four
Back to place and swing partner
Down the center and cast off two
All swing partners
Allemande left your corners all
Right and left around the hall

Other couples repeat in turn.

PLAIN QUADRILLE # 9

As called by Happy Hale

Figure One

MUSIC: *Golden Slippers*

On your heels and on your toes
Join your hands and around you go
The other way back you're going wrong

First couple right down the center and pass between the opposite two

The gent go right, the lady go left

Around the outside back to place

Balance to your corners and then your partners all

Take that corner lady and promenade the hall

First gentleman repeat the figure with his corner, then the second does the changes twice, and the other men in turn. To end the figure Happy calls

Right hand to your partners all and right and left around the hall.

Figure Two

MUSIC: *Hinkey Dinkey Parley Voo*

This figure was first done to this music in New London, Conn.

First couple around the outside, back to place

Swing your corners all

Cross your hands across the set and promenade the same

First gentleman repeats the figure with his corner as in the preceding number, then the other men do same in turn.

Figure Three

MUSIC: *Buffalo Gals*

First lady lead up to the right

Turn that gent with the right hand round

Back to partner and left hand around

Lady to the center and seven around

Swing your corners everyone

Leave her alone and swing your own

First gent lead up to the right

Turn that lady with your right hand round

Back to your partner and left hand around

Swing in the center and six around

Everybody shake 'er down

Dos a dos your corners all
Do the same with your own little doll
Allemande left with the lady on your left
And swing your partners all
The next lady and gent repeat, and the others in turn. After
    all have done the figure Happy calls
Every gentleman lead to the right
Swing that lady with all your might
And now that lady across the set
Every gentleman lead to the left
Swing the one that you swing best
All promenade.

BASKET QUADRILLE

First couple lead to the right, four hands around
Cross eight hands, gents bow the ladies know how and around
    you go
Right hands half around, left hands back
Swing the opposite lady
All swing partners
All promenade.

The same couple now repeats the changes with the other two
couples. Then the second couple goes through the changes, then
the third couple, then the last. In some localities it is the custom
for the second couple to start as soon as the first two begin the
changes with the last couple.

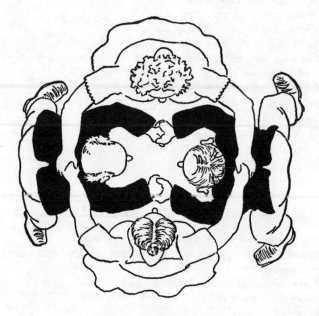

GENTS BOW——

Another way of doing this dance:

First four lead to the right and do the above changes with the
    side couples

Then the side couples lead to the right and perform the changes
    with the first four

The first four forward and do the changes

Then the side couples forward and do the changes.

AND LADIES KNOW HOW

If you're husky enough, you will perform *Gents bow, ladies know how* this way:

As the gents swing arms over the ladies' heads, they lower them back of the ladies' knees and lift their partners off the floor, basket-seat fashion. The ladies must be taken by surprise and spun violently to get the full effect of this figure.

As we said before but repeat now, just to re-nail our point: All square dances are not quadrilles, just as all country dances are not squares.

Darling Nellie Gray and The Girl I Left Behind Me are two square dances which originated in New York State. They were danced to countless tunes before a final version was settled upon and they were ready to migrate into New England. The country west of the Green Mountains and along the Berkshires happened to like these squares, but elsewhere they were regarded with contempt reserved for the foreigner. And the old folks thought them on a par with London Bridge Is Falling Down or any of the kids' games of the day. The newer generation found them fun to do, however, and so they became established throughout southern New England.

In Darling Nellie Gray four couples make up the set formed as for a plain quadrille. We'll give you the calls first and explain them afterwards.

DARLING NELLIE GRAY

MUSIC: *The Same*

First couple down the center, cast off six
Ladies to the right and the gents to the left
Give your right hand to your partner
While you balance all away
And you all swing your Darling Nellie Gray
Now allemande left with your corners all
And grand right and left around the hall.
The same couple down the center, cast off four
The ladies to the right and the gents carve the left

With your right hand to your partner
You will balance all away
And you all swing your Darling Nellie Gray
Now allemande left with your corners all
And grand allemande around the hall
The same couple down the center, cast off two
The ladies wing the right and the gents fly the left
Give your right hand to your partner
And balance all away
Then you all swing your Darling Nellie Gray
Now allemande left with your corners all
Eight hands twice around and back the other way

Only two of the calls should present any difficulty to experienced dancers. The first one is *cast off six*. Remember that you are in a square formation. The head couple walks down the center of the set toward the opposite couple. This couple obligingly moves apart to allow the first couple to pass between them. That is *cast off six*. The lady now promenades around the outside of the set to the right and her partner to the left. The next one, *Give your right hand to your partner and balance all away* is twice as easy as it sounds. You have done the same thing hundreds of times in Hull's Victory. The head couple, upon returning to place, join right hands, give left hands to their corners and balance four in line.

Cast off four. The head couple walks down the center as before. This time, however, the lady passes to the right between the opposite couple and the second couple. The gent goes to the left between the opposite and fourth couples. This change requires just a bit less time than casting off six, and to fill in the extra two or three seconds the head couple should attempt a few fancy steps.   That explains *the gents carve the left*. In *cast off two*, the head couple start down the center as before, the lady passing between the second couple and the gent between the fourth couple.

There are as many ways of dancing The Girl I Left Behind Me as there are callers who use the tune. The one that follows is becoming the most favored:

❧

GIRL I LEFT BEHIND ME

MUSIC: The Same

Head couple start and go through the chances twice. Then the second couple do them twice and so on.

Take your sweetie by the hand and promenade down the center
The lady goes right, the gent goes wrong
And all swing your corners.
The gents turn round and swing all around
With the girl you left behind you
Allemande left with the lady on your left
And promenade all with your own little doll

Another way of doing the dance is a bit more complex, but not alarmingly so:

First couple lead to the right, balance there so handy
Then pass right through and balance too
And swing that girl behind you.
Ladies grand chain
All promenade with the blushing maid
The girl you left behind you.

The first command of any difficulty is *pass right through and balance too*. To do it, the head and right hand couple execute a half right and left and balance back to back. Then those two gentlemen swing the lady behind them, who of course is the other man's partner. Still retaining this new partner and new position they are ready for the grand chain. After this, the two men who have been involved in the swinging and balancing exchange return to their partners and all promenade. The next couple then take their turn and so on until all have done the dance. The prompter will then sing out something like this:

Promenade all around the hall
You know where and I don't care
Throw her in the old armchair

And so, panting, you wait for the music to strike up a nice, easy contry dance.

PAT'NELLA

SOME CONTRYS
Hybrid Variety

Chapter V

IF you are an all-wool Yankee, you naturally call them *contry* dances. If you're just part-wool, you'll probably mis-hear them as *country* dances. And if you bother to look the word up, you'll find that *contra* is the term as it originated, suggesting, of course, the two "contrary" lines in the set-up. But, Mr. Webster and the rest notwithstanding, we are calling them . . . as we always have . . . contry dances.

To get the whole business straightened out once and for all, here's a little formula: *Contry* dances plus *quadrilles* equal *country* dances.

Varied as a handful of snowflakes, these dozen or so are really the hybrids that come under the category of neither jigs, reels, nor hornpipes. The variety comes not only in style, but in the ease or difficulty in doing the figures. For instance, you could probably toss off a Merry Dance, Pop Goes the Weasel, French Four or Wild Goose Chase *sans* rehearsal, and nobody would suspect! But it would take a Philadelphia lawyer to untangle a set of raw recruits undertaking a Money Musk, Hull's Victory or Patronella.

Perhaps the biggest pet wherever it is danced is the Morning Star, although it is a comparative new-comer. Some say that it sprang out of one of Vermont's Connecticut River towns; but Maine denies this. Probably other states will claim credit for its beginnings, but we'll let the scholars and historical G-men straighten that out. All we know is that Morning Star runs neck-and-neck in popularity with Lady Walpole's Reel and Portland Fancy. And here's why:

MORNING STAR

MUSIC: Rakes of Mallon if 2/4 time is preferred, Haste to the Wedding if 6/8 time is favored, as it is in some places.

Contry Formation . . . . Six or Eight Couples in a Set

Give right hand to partner, balance and swing	8 bars
Give left hand to partner, balance and swing	8 "
Down the center and back	8 "
Cast off, right and left	8 "

First, third and fifth couples start the dance.

Downeast is the favorite stamping ground, so to speak, for Lady of the Lake, another of these contrys. Not hard to learn, it is nevertheless a giddy affair and had best be shunned by the unsteady whirlers. Not only do you, as first, third and fifth couples, balance swing the couple below (as in Lady Walpole's Reel), but immediately you duplicate the figure with your own partner! This is apple pie for the real Yankee gals whose aim and ambition has ever been to swing their partners off the floor and right out straight.

On this same theme, well do we remember the ballroom initiation of one of our best friends at the age of thirteen. It was the Lady of the Lake, with his mother for a partner. In all blue-eyed innocence he joined in with these avid Yankee swingers and by the time he reached the head of the set, he had been wafted from the floor more than once. The climax came with "swing your partners." He took off from the maternal side like a plane from a navy carrier, zoomed up onto the stage and made a one-point landing among the musicians' feet. Unable to steady himself even then, he rolled half the length of the stage and ended in a final unconscious embrace of the prompter's legs. When the prompter disentangled himself and stood up, he announced: "There now, folks. is what *I* call real swingin'."

LADY OF THE LAKE

MUSIC: Speed the Plow

Contry Formation . . . . *Six or Eight Couples in a Set*

First couple cross over, balance and swing the one below	8 bars
First couple balance and swing partner in the center	8 "
First couple down the center and back	8 "
Cast off, right and left	8 "

Third and fifth couples also start the dance.

❧

Another dance that would make a corpse shuffle his feet in his coffin is Money Musk. They say that this was first danced on the village green of Moneymusk on the river Don in Aberdeenshire. Since it was first danced, there have been as many variations on the original tune as there have been fiddlers to play them. And there have been changes in the dance figures, too. Originally the first call was "Right hand to partner, swing once and a half around." Since this walk-around business proved a bit slow, the young blades of fifty or sixty years ago revamped it. The oldsters were properly horrified, but finally gave in, the way they always do. The new version holds to this day. Moderately difficult to do, Money Musk is perfectly learnable, with a little concentration:

MONEY MUSK

MUSIC: The Same

Contry Formation . . . . Six or Eight Couples in a Set

Swing partner in the center	8 bars
Each go below one couple and forward six	4 "
Right hand to partner, turn three-quarters round	4 "
Forward six	4 "
Right hand to partner, turn three-quarters round to place	4 "
Right and left	8 "

Fourth couple also starts the dance.

Patronella . . . Pat'nella in simon-pure vernacular . . . is something different. It is one of those dances which demand split-second timing; so, doing this in ordinary fashion results in a slipshod, inartistic affair. Hence those whose timing is not drawn to a fine bead had better just sit by in awe and admiration . . . or, better still, just go out and have a drink.

Of course, the old folks really *danced* the Pat'nella. There was Isaac Dunn, for instance, a dancing master in his day . . . he was always at least four inches off the floor when the music stopped! Our grandmothers still talk about the Pat'nella celebrities of their time, how they used this dance as a showpiece for their cloggings and pigeon's wings. While we can't boast nearly so many fine fancy dancers, there are still some who can manage a Pat'nella creditably. We have seen them clog with arms akimbo or snap their fingers and yelp with excitement. Obviously this is not a dance for the pickle-faces.

To a good many "G fiddlers" the tune was a bit complicated; The Girl I Left Behind Me or Finnegan's Wake were often substituted. But a crowd of real Pat'nella dancers would never be satisfied with anything but the original music.

PAT'NELLA

MUSIC: The Same

Contry Formation . . . . *Six or Eight Couples in a Set*

First couple advance to center of set, turn round to
  the right and balance   4 bars
   (This time you are balancing up and down the
     hall.)
Turn round to right and balance again   4 "
   (This time you are on the opposite side of the
     line from where you started.)
Turn round to right and balance again   4 "
Turn round to right and balance in place   4 "
Down the center with your partner and back   8 "
Cast off, right and left   8 "

HULL'S VICTORY

Hull's Victory is another pet. As you've already guessed, this dance is typically American, and it could no more be left out of an evening's program than the stars could be dropped from the American flag.

We've heard our grandmother tell of a man hereabouts by the name of Wilson, who danced and fiddled with considerable "know how." Whenever Hull's Victory was called for, he would insist on playing or dancing it in an old, forlorn seersucker coat which he said he had been wearing when the news came of the victory of Hull's *Constitution*.

Today's way of dancing Hull's Victory is a bit different from the original version. Many of the oldsters frown on it as we do it now, forgetting, of course, that they themselves were the very ones who shuffled Money Musk about to suit their own fancy fifty odd years ago! There's no doubt that our Hull's Victory is going to last because it is an exhilarating dance without being an exhausting one . . . a swell ingredient for long life. (*See following page*).

BALANCE—

HULL'S VICTORY

MUSIC: The Same

Contry Formation . . . . Six or Eight Couples in a Set

Give right hand to partner, left to opposite and balance four in line	4 bars
Turn the opposite twice around with left hand	4 "
Right hand to partner, left to opposite, balance four in line	4 "
Turn your partner in the center	4 "
Down the center and back	8 "
Cast off, right and left	8 "

First, third and fifth couples start the dance.

FOUR IN LINE

When a couple arrive at the head of the set, they wait during one repetition of a figure before starting at the head. The couple arriving at the foot also wait one repetition before they begin their way up toward the head.

Among the contrys which you can do right off, blind-folded, almost, is the French Four. Don't ask us if it is really French, for we don't know. Neither does anyone else. But certainly in towns having a high percentage of Canucks, this dance is a favorite. Probably it is Canadian in origin; or, if not, it must surely have come over here via Canada.

This dance always used to be put in a program as a breather between two high-powered numbers, since it contains plenty of balancing and very little swinging.

FRENCH FOUR

MUSIC: Turkey in the Straw

Contry Formation . . . . Six or Eight Couples in a Set

Balance partner and cross over	4	bars
Go below one couple	4	"
Balance again	4	"
Cross back to place	4	"
Down the center with partner and back	8	"
Cast off, right and left	8	"

Third and fifth couples also start the dance.

Still calmer is the Wild Goose Chase, name to the contrary. Here is plenty of balancing and no swinging whatever! This is probably why hardly more than cambric enthusiasm is shown today for both this dance and the French Four.

However, for those who want to run a country dance with no foxtrots or moderns spliced in as breathers, both these dances will come in very handy.

WILD GOOSE CHASE

MUSIC: *The Same*

Contry Formation . . . . *Six or Eight Couples in a Set*

First couple cross over before music starts

First and third couples join hands with partners and balance in center toward each other. (Second couple stand like lighthouses) — 4 bars

First couple walk behind second lady and take third couple's place. At the same time third couple walks behind second gent and takes first couple's place. (Second couple still stand like lighthouses) — 4 "

These two couples balance again — 4 "

First and third couples return in same way to original places — 4 "

First couple down center and back — 8 "

Cast off, right and left — 8 "

(Remember gent is on lady's side, from original crossing over before music began.)

Head couple continue, dancing with fourth, fifth, sixth, etc., couples.

Each head couple cross over before they begin their performance. When they reach the foot of the set they cross over to their respective sides.

And now comes the dance that everybody either knows by experience or rumor . . . Pop Goes the Weasel. So simple that newcomers can join right in, and hilarious enough to make the Tired Business

Man forget all about Overhead and Statistics, this dance is rightfully one of the most popular of its kind. In many sections of this country it is done in square formation, but the Devil hates holy water no less than the Yankees hate the thought of Pop Goes the Weasel done as anything but a contry.

POP GOES THE WEASEL

MUSIC: The Same

Contry Formation . . . . Six or Eight Couples in a Set

First couple down the outside and back	8 bars
Down center and back	8 "
Three hands around with next lady	8 "
(Couple form arch and POP lady through to music.)	
Three hands around with that lady's partner	8 "
(Same couple form arch and POP gent through to music.)	
Third and fifth couples also start the dance.	

Other popular ones among the less boisterous contrys were the Twin Sisters, so named probably because the ladies dance together much of the time; and Ladies' Triumph, sometimes known as Katy's Rambles. Both these dances came from the north of Ireland. Most men will agree after dancing Katy's Rambles that Katy most certainly does travel and that it isn't such a cinch to follow the wench, either.

THE HOLMES BROTHERS' MERRY DANCE

Perhaps one of the happiest numbers of this group is the Merry Dance. Everyone seems to like this one no matter which way he believes it should be danced. Of the several versions, we like the one which originated with the Holmes brothers in Stoddard, New Hampshire. They wrote the music for it, too. These boys are contemporary Yankees, and their dance is loyally done in all of the surrounding towns. On one occasion not many years ago, the Merry Dance became part of Stoddard's history. It was the night of the *"great blizzard"* (not the Great Blizzard of '88). The snow began to swirl off Pitcher Mountain, and the dancers were forced to stay the night in the town hall. The dance went on as the snow piled up against the windows. Nobody could get home. At the turn of dawn, when the oil lamps were blown out, the orchestra struck up the Holmes brothers' Merry Dance. The dancers stepped this one out until finally the cornetist rebelled. Putting down his instrument he shouted, "What the hell is this, anyway, a dance or a blank-blank overture?" Thereafter the dance was nicknamed The Stoddard Overture. And now, when someone suggests a Stoddard Overture, why don't you ask him if he remembers the night when . . . .?

MERRY DANCE

MUSIC: *The Same*

Contry Formation . . . . *Six or Eight Couples in a Set*

First couple cross over, first lady down outside and back with second gent; first gent down the outside and back with second lady at same time	8 bars
Same four join hands, down center four and back	8 "
Cast off, ladies chain	8 "
Half promenade	4 "
Half right and left	4 "

Third and fifth couples start the dance at the same time.

Next to Pat'nella, the most complicated of these hybrids is The Tempest. The following is the simplest version we know, and the versions are many, even in this part of the country:

THE TEMPEST

MUSIC: *The Same*

Contry Formation . . . . *Six or Eight Couples in a Set*

First two couples down center and back, four abreast	8 bars
First couple balance the third couple	4 "
Four hands around with that couple	4 "
Same two ladies chain	8 "

Same two couples down center four abreast and do the other changes with the next couple, and so on until all have done the figure.

This last, The Arkansas Traveler, was once near the top of the list of favorites. Then it fell on evil days for some unknown reason, and only recently has it started to boomerang into favor. The story of its origin goes like this: Once there was a smart tin peddler who used to hawk his shiny wares up and down the Connecticut River valley. He had an admirable drawl and was a perfect bull's-eye shot with a mouthful of plug. On the strength of this he told folks he hailed from Ar-Kansas. This dance was dedicated, they say, to this nameless "Ar-Kansan" and was given about twice the number of calls usual to contrys, probably to symbolize the peddler's wanderings:

ARKANSAS TRAVELER

MUSIC: The Same. Play Straight Through; Do Not Repeat Either Strain.

Contry Formation . . . . Six or Eight Couples in a Set

First three couples forward and balance	4	bars
Six hands half around	4	"
Forward again and balance	4	"
Six hands half around to place	4	"
First four cross right hands half round, swing partners	8	"
Left hand back to place	4	"
First couple swing	4	"
First couple down center and back	8	"
Cast off, right and left	8	"

Fourth couple also start this dance.

You will notice that it requires forty-eight bars of music to perform the steps of this dance, instead of the customary thirty-two. To make the music fit the steps it should be played straight through, ignoring the repeat signs at the end of the eighth and sixteenth measures.

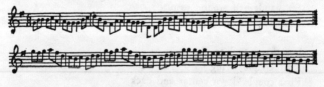

JIG

SMALL POTATOES AND FEW IN A HILL

THANKS TO
THE IRISH

SOME JIGS

Chapter VI

WHENEVER we think of jigs, a certain green island across the water invariably comes into our minds, for we in this country have always preferred the Irish jigs to either the English or the Scotch ones. The influx of Paddies into our mill towns might have had a lot to do with our preference, but probably we'd have taken to the Irish ones anyway. Like the Irish, they are the most joyous and carefree of the three; even the names . . . just to hear them makes you want to get up and dance. Listen: Smash the Window, Shoe the Donkey, Patrick's Pot, Pretty Girl Milking Her Cow, Petticoat Swish, Strop the Razor, The Growling Old Woman, There's Whiskey in the Jar, and Barney, Leave the Girls Alone.

Jigs are probably our oldest dances. Many of them can be traced back to the days of druids when the Irish held annual feasts that lasted six days. On the three days before our November first and the two days following, it was customary for Mr. and Mrs. Patrick Uppercrust, with bard and harpist, to come from far and near to the castle of their king. The Gaelic name for the festival was Feis (pronounced fesh, we think). There were grand competitions in all kinds of music and dancing, and the jigs were danced there as solos by a man or woman, a form seldom seen nowadays.

The personal history of the English jig is quite a different story. In the early period of the English stage, a jig, accompanied by playing and dancing, was the common wind-up to a play, and was either spoken or sung by the clown. It was only performed, however, when the audience called for it. In old pictures, Tarleton is represented playing jigs on his tabor; the music for Tarleton's jig is still preserved.

Kemp's Jig is spoken of, not as a ballad, but as a dance.

> *A hall! a hall!*
> *Room for the spheres, the orbes celestial*
> *Will* daunce *Kemp's Jigge.*

Kemp's jig is still extant. Kemp, by the way, was a celebrated actor who said of himself once that he spent his life "in a mad rounde of jigges."

The haunting melodies of the Irish jigs spring out

of the old Irish scale which consisted of five notes, corresponding to the black keys of our piano. Jigs were divided into single and double jigs according to the number of beats to the bar, and the true jig steps are similar to the steps in the Scotch reels.

Closely allied is the planxty: music written for the harp in a much slower time. Everybody knows the good old tune, Irish Washerwoman, but who would ever suspect that this, one of our most popular jigs, was originally played in very slow 3/4 time! A very ancient air it is, once known as Tatter the Road.

IRISH WASHERWOMAN

Form Contry Line-up . . . . . . Six or Eight Couples in a Set

First three couples forward and back	4	bars
Turn partners half around with right hand	4	"
Same six forward and back again	4	"
Turn partners to place with right hand	4	"
First two couples down center and back	8	"
First couple cast off, right and left four	8	"

Fourth couples also start the dance.

Munster jigs were originally written for the bagpipe, and a list as long as a lover's kiss could be made of the tunes written by and for the pipers. Paddy O'Rafferty, Larry Grogan, Mulcahy's, Mulvaney's, Kitty O'Neil's and Lannigan's Ball, are a few.

When Irish pipers were once as famous as those of
Scotland, Irish soldiers used to march to jig music
played very slowly on the bagpipes. And every little
village had its piper who played for the villagers to
dance on the green. After an hour or more of dancing
the piper would dig a small hole in the ground and
strike up a tune which was then called Gather Up
the Money. This was a polite and still musical way
of hinting that those who dance must pay the piper.
When the dance was over, the piper would scoop in
his haul which had accumulated coin by coin as the
dancers passed by. Today this tune is known as The
Blackberry Blossom.

During the George VI Coronation ceremonies, the
director of one of the London military bands mentioned that the tune now known as The British Gren-
adiers was originally an old Irish folk tune. Which,
of course, points to one more development in the
evolution of the old Irish jigs.

Real Irish jig steps are seldom seen today in this
country. Once in a while a Paddy just landed will
do a step, the nearest approach to which are our clog
and double shuffle. Some people claim that the pigeon's wing is of Irish origin, but the point is debat-
able.

Besides the jigs which are Yankee variations of the Irish folk dances, we also have a few which sprang from our own soil. The Jefferson and Liberty, for instance, is supposed to have come out of Maine:

THE JEFFERSON AND LIBERTY

MUSIC: The Same, or Top of Cork Road

Form Contry Line-up . . . . . . Six or Eight Couples in a Set

First two couples four hands around and back	8 bars
Cross right hands half around	4 "
Left hands back to place	4 "
First couple down center and back	8 "
Cast off, right and left	8 "

Third and fifth couples also start the dance.

Years ago, Vermont's favorite was The Green Mountain Jig. This is a grand number which really deserves to be more popular than it is at present.

THE GREEN MOUNTAIN JIG

[ALSO KNOWN AS GREEN MOUNTAIN VOLUNTEERS]

MUSIC: Haste to the Wedding or Green Mountain Boys

Form Contry Line-up . . . . . . Six or Eight Couples in a Set

First, third and every other couple cross over before music starts.	
Right hand line chassez down the hall and back, left hand line balance and swing at same time	8 bars
Right hand line balance and swing, other line chassez	8 "
Those that crossed over, down center and back	8 "
Cast off, right and left	8 "

Finnegan's Wake and Mulligan's Wake are still pretty common tunes in New England, although in Ireland they are played only at wakes . . . those curious mixtures of sorrow and gaiety.

Words as well as dance steps went with many of the well-known tunes. The best known were St. Patrick was a Gentleman, Paddy Duffy's Cart, The Low Backed Car, Rory O'More and Garry Owen. Here is a description of Rory O'More:

RORY O'MORE

MUSIC: The Same

Form Contry Line-up . . . . . . Six or Eight Couples in a Set

First couple cross over, down outside below two	4 bars
Up center, cross to place and cast off	4 "
Give right hand to partner and balance	4 "
Step two steps to right by each other; join left hand and balance again	4 "
Swing contry corners	8 "
Balance partner	4 "
Swing partner to place	4 "

Fourth couple also start dance.

The Galway Piper is a popular tune among the Women's Club choruses of the country, which air, old-time fiddlers and dancers will recognize as the Rakes of Mallon. When sung with the proper spirit, it doesn't take a great deal of imagination to picture an Irish jig, trimmed with excited whoops and brandishings of blackthorn or shillalagh.

Here are some of the common jigs danced in New England. The first cannot possibly be left out of an evening's program:

CHORUS JIG

MUSIC: *The Same*

Form Contry Line-up . . . . . . Six or Eight Couples in a Set

First couple down the outside and back	8 bars
Down center and back	8 "
Cast off, swing contry corners	8 "
Forward six	4 "
Swing partner in center	4 "

(In some sections of New England, this last change goes like this: Turn partner to place with right hand.)

Fourth couple also start the dance.

SWING CONTRY CORNERS

LARRY O'GAFF

MUSIC: The Same

Form Contry Line-up . . . . . . *Six or Eight Couples in a Set*

First two couples right and left	8 bars
First couple down center, turn half round and back	8 "
Cast off, ladies chain	8 "
All forward and back, and key couples cross to place	8 "

Third and fifth couples also start the dance.

THE GRACES

MUSIC: Isle of Skye or The Graces

Form Contry Line-up . . . . . . *Six or Eight Couples in a Set*

First three couples forward and back	4 bars
Chassez half around to left	4 "
Balance six again	4 "
Chassez round to place	4 "
First four cross right hands half around	4 "
Same four swing their partners	4 "
Left hands back to place	4 "
Swing partners	4 "
First couple down center and back	8 "
Cast off, right and left	8 "

Fourth couple also start the dance.

ST. PATRICK'S DAY IN THE MORNING

MUSIC: The Same

Form Contry Line-up . . . . . . Six or Eight Couples in a Set

Head couple down the outside and back	8 bars
Same two down center and back	8 "
Cast off and forward six	4 "
Six hands half around	4 "
Forward six again	4 "
Six hands half around to place	4 "
First two couples cross right hands half round	4 "
Left hands back to place	4 "
Ladies chain	8 "

Garry Owen is particularly well remembered in the New Hampshire towns of Stoddard and Nelson. It was the favorite tune of the gallant but foolhardy General Custer, and was always played when the young cavalrymen under his command left the fort for reprisals against the Indians. A month before the battle of Little Big Horn, young Eldorado Robb, a native of Stoddard, New Hampshire, was transferred, at his own request, to General Custer's command. That was the last ever heard from him. Every time that this tune was played, his cousins living over in Nelson would be reminded of him and never fail to recount the story of the brave Robb who died with his boots on.

SWING YOUR PARTNER

A GIFT FROM THE SCOTS

SOME REELS

Chapter VII

In our opinion any country dance evening is a flop which doesn't include at least one Scotch reel in its program. Like the Scots, themselves, reels are energetic pieces, guaranteed sure-cures for everything from the blues to poor circulation. But if there is any Scotch in your blood, even the first measures of Five Mile Chase or Where's My Other Foot will probably send you entirely daft!

About the most popular of the early ones in this country is Lady Walpole's Reel. Generally it was known as the married man's favorite because of the little time spent in the company of your own partner. Besides the nickname, throughout New England the dance is variously called Boston Fancy, Lady Washington's Reel and Speed the Plow. But the changes are the same, and they, rather than the name, are what count.

More stories about this dance seem to be floating around than any we know of. There's one we always liked about the famous wedding reel at Vinal Haven, Maine. In this settlement of Scotch granite workers, the old custom of dancing right after a wedding ceremony was observed. Sometimes the dance was held in the new home, sometimes at the dominie's or in a public gathering place, and the bridegroom and blushing bride always led off the first reel.

This particular dance celebrated the marriage of a popular couple, who led off with a long and boisterous Lady Walpole's Reel. Instead of swinging her off her feet, as was orthodox, the men decided that bussing the bride would be a pleasant variation to the theme. (Bussing: kissing.) Can you picture the poor lady after going through a dozen or more sets of bristly whiskers?

Today (without the bussing variation), Lady Walpole's Reel is danced at least once, and sometimes twice or three times, during an evening, competing for first place with the Plain Quadrille. Here's how it's done:

LADY WALPOLE'S REEL

MUSIC: *The Same*

Form Contry Line-up . . . . . . Six or Eight Couples in a Set

Before the music starts the first, third and every
other couple cross over.

Those that crossed over:

Balance and swing the couple below	8 bars
Down the center with partner and back	8 "
Cast off, ladies chain	8 "
Half promenade	4 "
Half right and left	4 "

Repeat, swinging the next couple, etc., until all have
done the changes.

One of the best known reels is Miss McLeod's.
It is also known as the Enterprise and Boxer, but
the Scotch name is undoubtedly the original title.
Here is the way New England steps it:

MISS McLEOD'S REEL

MUSIC: *The Same*

Form Contry Line-up . . . . . . Six or Eight Couples in a Set

First couple down the center, turn half round, back	8 bars
(Lady is now on gent's side of set and gent is on the lady's side.)	
Cast off, ladies chain	8 "
Promenade four	8 "
Forward and back	4 "
First couple cross over to place	4 "

Third and fifth couples also start the dance.

Fifty years ago no contry was in more demand than Devil's Dream, which bears a decided resemblance to Old Zip Coon. Some people say that the Devil was invented after Old Zip Coon, and others are just as certain that Old Zip is an outgrowth of the Devil. One school of thought is right, indeed; but which one, has never been decided.

For some unknown reason this dance (and also Speed the Plow) fail to click with the modern Yankee idea of what constitutes a good set. However, the tunes are still popular and are played a lot for many other contry dances.

All fiddlers are jealous of their accomplishments, you know, and it is an absolute impossibility to be accepted into their clan unless one can perform both Devil's Dream and Speed the Plow in a creditable manner, preferably with home-made variations. Old Theophilus (Parse) Ames used to say that a fiddler without his own version of Devil's Dream was of "as much account as a string of wampum in the Washington mint." Ames lived in Peterborough, New Hampshire, and was one of the finest fiddlers in his part of the country.

DEVIL'S DREAM

MUSIC: The Same

Form Contry Line-up . . . . . . *Six or Eight Couples in a Set*

Before the music starts, first couple cross over.

Down the outside and back   8 bars

(Foot couple up center and back at same time.)

First couple down center and back   8 bars

(Foot couple up outside and back at same time.)

First couple cast off, ladies chain   8 "

Right and left   8 "

Continue until all have done the figure.

Of the several contry dances which first appeared in the old-time operas, one popular survivor is the Opera Reel. In many parts of New England this dance is nearly as well liked as Lady Walpole's Reel; and with some people, like our neighbor, it is unquestionably the favorite. She is a barrel-waisted lady with considerable all-over displacement, who says that nothing beats Opera Reel in her estimation, but after the second trip down the center, she always spends the rest of the figure looking for a hired girl to breathe for her!

OPERA REEL

MUSIC: The Same

Form Contry Line-up . . . . . . *Six or Eight Couples in a Set*

Head couple down the outside and back   8 bars

Head couple down the center and back   8 "

Cast off, give right arm to partner and reel   8 "

(Partners link right arms and turn once around. Then the first gent reels the second lady with the left arm, then his partner with his right arm, then the head lady with left arm. His partner reels the opposite gent at same time.)

First couple balance and swing in the center   8 "

Fourth couple also start the dance.

Probably this next dance, the Virginia Reel, is universally familiar; every kid seems to know how to do it, no matter how little country dance training he has had, and for years it has been the common wind-up of an evening's program. Because it is so well known we are not going to list it here.

But we are presenting a more recent variation, as imported from the south, one which seems to fit the temper of modern times a great deal better. Hereabouts it is very popular and has entirely supplanted the old dance which never failed, when announced, to call forth groans and bored expressions. We first saw this new dance done at Antrim, New Hampshire, and watched it spread to the surrounding towns where it is often requested now three or four times in an evening! Dance history right under our noses, what?

VIRGINIA REEL

MUSIC: First part Irish Washerwoman, second part White Cockade, third part There'll Be a Hot Time in the Old Town Tonight.

Form Contry Line-up . . . . . . Six or Eight Couples in a Set

All forward and back	4 bars
Forward again and reel partner with right arm	4 "
Forward again and reel with left arm	4 "
All forward and back	4 "
All turn partners with right hand	4 "
All turn partners with left hand	4 "
All turn partners with both hands	4 "
All dos a dos with partner	4 "

Remainder of the dance is the same as the old style, with the head couple reeling their dizzy way down through the set, and up the center to the tune of the White Cockade. Then to the march, the head lady marches to the right followed by her line of ladies; head gent marches to the left followed by his line of gents. All join hands and up the center. Then all the others form an arch with their joined hands, while the head couple go down the center under the arch, to the bottom of the set, and become the foot couple. We dare say that this dance will survive and be enjoyed for many generations to come.

❧

Another grand one is Miss Brown's Reel. If you like to swing, don't miss this one:

MISS BROWN'S REEL

MUSIC: The Same

Form Contry Line-up . . . . . . *Six or Eight Couples in a Set*

First lady swing the second gent	4 bars
First gent swing the second lady	4 "
First couple down the center and back	8 "
Cast off, forward and back four	4 "
First gent swing partner	4 "
Right and left with second couple	8 "

Third and every other couple also start the dance.

RIGHT AND LEFT

In some sections Beaux of Albany is known as the Rosebud Reel, and that tune is often played for the following:

BEAUX OF ALBANY

MUSIC: The Same or Rosebud Reel

Form Contry Line-up . . . . . . Six or Eight Couples in a Set

First and second couples balance and swing partners	8	bars
Both couples down center and back; cast off	8	"
Cross right hands half around	4	"
Left hands back to place	4	"
Same couples right and left	8	"

Third and fifth couples also start the dance.

This next dance is one of our own invention which we first tried out on some "furriners" at a ski-dance in Nelson. They survived.

HAPPY VALLEY REEL

MUSIC: The Rival

Form Contry Line-up . . . . . . *Six or Eight Couples in a Set*

Before the music starts, first, third and every other couple cross over. The couples that crossed over **now:**

Give right hand to next below, balance and reel	8 bars
Give left hand to same, balance and reel	8 "
Those that crossed over down the outside and up the center	8 "
Cast off, promenade across and back	8 "

Back in our youth a white-bearded Civil War veteran used to tell us this story, the authenticity of which we don't guarantee. During the Revolution, parts of the colonies were hot-beds of Toryism, especially along the Schoharie River and adjacent country. The MacDonald Rangers were a group of the king's sympathizers, buckskinned and war-painted. For months these "blue-eyed Indians" swooped down on the defenseless outposts until their name became sour indeed to the hard-pressed colonists. After many massacres, ably assisted by Joseph Brant's Iroquois, the Rangers were caught and soundly trounced.

MacDonald's group had their pipers along with them and their theme song was All the Blue Bonnets Over the Border, which they would play as they were ready to carry out a little massacre. To this day MacDonald has been a bloody name in our history, and, according to our white-bearded friend, his reel is not everywhere popular even at this date.

But there are some reels which transcend all hard feelings, whose very names make us grin: The Auld Maid Wad be Married, My Mither Aye Glowerin' O'er Me, Kiss Me Sweetly, Saw Ye Ma Wee Thing?, Looney MacTwolter, Come Under My Plaidie and Good Mornin' to Your Nightcap.

OUT OF THE DOLDRUMS

SOME HORNPIPES

Chapter VIII

ENTER England, now, with her contribution, the hornpipe, a dance which probably wouldn't have been invented but for that country's great sea tradition. Exactly when or where it originated, nobody really knows, but legend has it that it was invented about four centuries ago aboard an English boat, stranded somewhere in the doldrums of the South Atlantic.

And what a set-up for an invention: weeks on end with no wind to stir the sails, and a boatload of sailors weary of it all. With the Welshman on board, there was some hope of a little relief. Besides piping all hands to grog, he had concocted a few catchy tunes on the hornpipe, that curious instrument with horns on both ends. As he sat and tootled in a bit of shade on the deck, the sailors danced. Not really danced, you understand; just improvised a few figures in the only medium they knew. They climbed an imaginary rope, looked out to sea first with the right hand to the forehead and then with the left, lurching as if in heavy weather, and now and then they gave a rhythmic tug fore and aft to their blue breeches. So that was the first hornpipe, right out of the doldrums.

And when the wind at last did blow again to send the ship scudding into port, there probably was a crew pretty well pleased to present the Sailors' Hornpipe to the tavern tipplers along the waterfront. Easy to catch on to, and offering lots of chance for new figures, sailors from other ships, and the lasses that loved them, were soon joining in.

The dance spread along the coast towns like quicksilver. Variations were many; there were Liverpool, Dundee, Newcastle and many more.

And there was Fisher's Hornpipe, one of the best, and still a popular number today:

FISHER'S HORNPIPE

MUSIC: *The Same*

Form Contry Line-up . . . . . . *Six or Eight Couples in a Set*

First couple down the outside and back	8 bars
Down the center and back	8 "
Six hands around	8 "
Right and left four	8 "

Fourth couple also start the dance.

The Irish, too, got interested and wrote and danced their own brands of hornpipe with characteristic gusto.

IRISH HORNPIPE

MUSIC: Peter Street

Form Contry Line-up . . . . . . Six or Eight Couples in a Set

First couple balance	4	bars
Down center	4	"
Balance at foot of set	4	"
Up center and cast off	4	"
First four cross right hands half around	4	"
Left hands back	4	"
Right and left four	8	"

Third and fifth couples also start the dance.

Then, of course, America. During the War of 1812, probably a good three centuries after the origin of the dance, the Constitution Hornpipe was written:

CONSTITUTION HORNPIPE

MUSIC: The Same

Form Contry Line-up . . . . . . Six or Eight Couples in a Set

First couple cross over before music begins.

Forward and back six	4	bars
Six hands half around	4	"
First and second couples, ladies chain	8	"
Same two couples, half promenade	4	"

Same two couples, half right and left to place   4 bars
Forward and back six   4 "
Swing to places   4 "
(Give right hand to partner and turn half way
round to where you started from.)
Second couple up the outside to head of set.
Fourth couple also cross over and start the dance.

Camptown Hornpipe came along in the covered wagon days when lots of Yankees were leaving their rocky farms for the flower-pot soil of the west. Democratic Rage Hornpipe bespeaks our political life when torchlight parades were rife. Red Lion Hornpipe probably was the specialty of an old New England Inn, along with deep-dish pork pie and beet pickles. Then came the Arctic, suggestive of our exploration days.

And the Lamplighter's, which represents the period when our towns really got settled:

LAMPLIGHTER'S HORNPIPE

MUSIC: The Same

Form Contry Line-up . . . . . . Six or Eight Couples in a Set

First couple cross over, balance three in line   4 bars
(They go between the second and third couples
and face out. Join hands with same two
couples and balance three on a side.)

Swing the right hand person	4 bars
(Gent swings lady to his right, lady swings gent to her right.)	
Balance again as before	4 "
Swing left hand person	4 "
Down center with partner and back	8 "
Cast off, right and left	8 "

Fourth couple also start the dance.

BALANCE THREE IN LINE

And there were more American ones, as American as Caleb Catlum: Cincinnati, Delaware, Niagara, Oyster River and Saratoga. But how come Good for the Tongue, Quindaro, Tiger, Brewer's Horse, Maid in the Pumproom? Nobody knows.

Cincinnati Hornpipe, was the tune which Mellie Dunham, Maine's famous fiddler, brought back to popularity. It was a thrilling sight to hear Mellie bowing this piece close to the bridge to give it that loud and penetrating tone which always picks up the spirit of any dance hall.

CINCINNATI HORNPIPE

MUSIC: The Same

Form Contry Line-up . . . . . . Six or Eight Couples in a Set

First two couples balance, half right and left	8 bars
Balance again, half right and left to place	8 "
First couple down center and back	8 "
Cast off, right and left	8 "

Third and fifth couples also start the dance.

The list of hornpipes named in honor of the men who either wrote or first played them is as long as a bread line. The ones most heard now are Durang's, Ned Kendall's, Douglas' Favorite, Eliot's, Rickett's and Vinton's.

DURANG'S HORNPIPE

MUSIC: The Same

Form Contry Line-up . . . . . . Six or Eight Couples in a Set

First lady balance second gent	4 bars
Swing partner	4 "
First gent balance second lady	4 "
Swing partner	4 "
First couple down center and back	8 "
Cast off, right and left	8 "

Third and fifth couples also start the dance.

RICKETT'S HORNPIPE

MUSIC: The Same

Form Contry Line-up . . . . . . Six or Eight Couples in a Set

First six balance and turn half round	8 bars
Balance again and turn to places	8 "
First couple down center and back	8 "
Cast off and ladies chain	8 "

Fourth couple also start the dance.

VINTON'S HORNPIPE

MUSIC: The Same

Form Contry Line-up . . . . . . Six or Eight Couples in a Set

First lady balance to first and second gents at same time	4 bars
Three hands around with same	4 "
First gent balance first and second ladies	4 "
Three hands around	4 "
First couple down center and back	8 "
Cast off, right and left	8 "

And there's the Black Eagle, too, supposed to have been written by David Rizzio, private secretary to Mary, Queen of Scots. It is a good tune, and somehow we feel that if Lord Darnley and the others who did away with poor David, had only allowed him a few minutes with his pipe, his life would have been saved. But then, they were impulsive fellows in that day.

And speaking of playing hornpipes, we are reminded of the time when the Munsonville, New Hampshire, orchestra was practising one summer night. The windows were open and the music attracted several camp boys who edged into the back row of the hall. Finally, one of the boys asked the violin player for his fiddle, and soon everybody had stopped playing to listen to the youngster. After several Brahms concertos and some Bach and Beethoven, one of the men inquired if he could play any hornpipes.

"No," the boy replied chyly, "I only play the violin."

POLKA-MANIA

AND THE ROUND DANCE ERA

Chapter IX

'Tis sweet on summer eve to rove
By the banks of the river Tolka,
But the joys of life but little prove
Unless you dance the Polka.
Oh! Won't you dance the Polka?
Oh! Can't you dance the Polka?
The joys of life but little prove
Unless you dance the Polka.

STOREKEEPERS sang the words between customers.
Young ladies hummed the tune to an unappreciative
moon. Country philosophers interrupted their whit-
tling long enough to try a measure or two. Everywhere people asked, *Oh! Won't you dance the Polka?*
And all because a Bohemian tavern wench had heard
good news from her lover in the Austrian army.

As she read the letter she sang and stamped and kicked, and Neruda, the local musician of Elbsteinitz, laid down his beer, noted her joyous antics, and made a bee-line for home where he wrote the music to the first polka.

The craze for the dance spread like a drop of dye in a tub of water. Hats and streets were named for it, and before long many an inn was inviting patronage with its sign "Polka Arms." It hopped the Atlantic to New England and threatened to eclipse forever the well-established squares and contrys. Everywhere the dance floors creaked to the tunes of "Genuine Polka," Heel and Toe Polka, the Polka Redowa, Polka Mazourka and other in-laws of the family.

The time was ripe, to be sure, for the introduction of a brisk, carefree round dance. The only ones in vogue were the old style waltz (which, though lively enough, allowed progress in only one direction) and the gallopade, which had little of the abandon of its modern derivative, the galop.

But, despite the fine reception it received, there were some standpatters who condemned it and tried to stop its spread. For all the good it did, they might as well have told the wind to stop blowing.

The editors of the ILLUSTRATED LONDON NEWS, a tried and true chronicle of the day, were, for instance, openly disdainful of it, and for months after its London debut, columns were filled with sarcastic editorials and cartoons ridiculing the importation. It was described as a "hybrid confusion of Scotch lilt, Irish jig and Bohemian waltz, which needs only to be seen once to be avoided for ever."

In spite of these diatribes, the dance kept growing in popularity until the editors, who must not then, as now, disregard what is news, capitulated, and this is what they printed on May 11, 1844:

> "The Polka begins with an introduction and consists of five figures. Of these, the heel and toe step, which was the most characteristic feature of the dance, has been abandoned probably owing to the difficulty in executing it properly, which generally caused it to result in the dancers' stamping their own heels upon other people's toes. We would observe that La Polka is a noiseless dance; there is no stamping of heels, toes, or kicking of legs in sharp angles forward. This may do very well at the threshold of a Bohemian *auberge*, but it is inadmissable in the salons of London. As now danced by us it is elegant, graceful and fascinating in the extreme; it is replete with opportunities of showing care and attention to your partner in assisting her through its performance."

The tempo of the dance was originally that of a military march played rather slowly. In later years it was performed somewhat faster, and more in the spirit of a waltz or galop.

THE POLKA

Music in 2/4 Time. For Gents: Waltz Position

The left foot must be raised to the side of the right ankle
Spring on right foot and at the same time slide the left
    foot to side, count 1
Close right foot to left foot, count 2

Step to side with left foot, count 3
Rest, count 4, all this to 1 bar
Repeat to the right, always starting with the raise or hop
Spring on left foot, and at the same time slide the right
    foot to side, count 1
Close left foot to right, count 2
Step to side with right foot, count 3
Rest, count 4, all this to 1 bar
Repeat all, using each foot alternately to begin the step.
The lady performs the same steps as the gent except that
    the feet are reversed, starting with the right foot instead
    of the left.

It must be remembered that a complete revolution requires two polka steps, one with the left foot first and the other with the right foot first, ending with the weight on the right foot. The reverse movement is the same as the other, except that in starting on each revolution, the gent steps back with the left foot, drawing his partner round, right foot first in the same direction as his left foot is going. The entire movement either way is facilitated by bending the head slightly in the direction of the out-stepping foot, left and right alternately.

Some dance instructors claim that there is no hopping in the dance, although its character is staccato. Many do not encourage this step in adult classes, although teaching it to children. If omitted, you should raise and lower your body on first the right toe, then the left.

A few years after the Polka's introduction into New England, the Heel-and-Toe Polka came in. It soon became the most popular number on the program.

What is believed to be the original tune for the dance was the Cracowvienne Polka. It came to this country under several aliases, the most prevalent, at least in the New Hampshire towns, being I Had A Bonnet Trimmed with Blue.

Goodnow's Orchestra of East Sullivan, New Hampshire, known for its ability and originality, introduced what was termed in those pre-crooning days, a startling innovation. At the second time through the tune the orchestra laid down their instruments and burst forth with this catchy, if not too well polished ditty:

> *Oh I had a bonnet trimmed with blue.*
> *Why don't you wear it? So I do.*
> *I do wear it when I can*
> *And go to the ball with a handsome man.*

Chorus

> *Hi Billy Martin, Tiptoe Jim,*
> *Here's the way the polk' begins,*
> *First your heel and then your toe*
> *That's the way the polka goes.*

What will mother say to me
When I come home with a broken knee?
I'll tell my mother to hold her tongue
For she did the same when she was young.

Chorus

Hi Billy Martin, Tiptoe Jim,
Here's the way the polk' begins,
First your heel and then your toe
That's the way the polka goes.

The dancers went mad. Everyone sang with the orchestra and insisted on numerous repetitions. Everywhere that Mr. Goodnow and his boys went, I Had a Bonnet Trimmed With Blue had to be performed.

Today the Heel and Toe has lost its popularity except in neighborhoods where there are lots of Finns, Scandinavians and Poles. Curiously enough, these people have never let it die. Through their interest, a slow revival is becoming evident as more and more Yankees attend the Finnish dances at Troy, Fitzwilliam, New Ipswich and Newport, New Hampshire, and the towns along the Black River Valley in Vermont, where this is still a favorite.

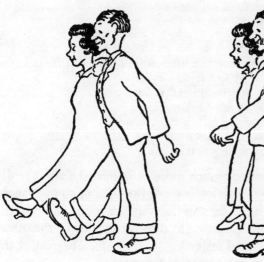

HEEL AND TOE

HEEL-AND-TOE POLKA

This can be danced in two positions; either the waltz, or open position (that is, standing beside partner nearest hands joined, lady to the gent's right). The directions given below are for the waltz position. Count 4 to a measure.

Place left heel to side, toe raised, count 1, 2
Place left toe on floor back of right heel, count 3, 4
Raise and lower on right heel (or hop) and at the same time
Slide left foot to side, count 1
Close right foot to left, count 2
Step to side with left foot, count 3

Rest, turning half to right, count 4
Repeat reversed, like this:
Place right heel to side, toe raised, count 1, 2
Place right toe on floor back of left heel, count 3, 4
Raise and lower on left heel (or hop) and at the same time
Slide right foot to side, count 1
Close left foot to right, count 2
Step right foot to side, count 3
Rest, turning half to right, count 4
Repeat both movements once each. Then make 8 polka
steps turning to the right.

This sounds much more complicated than it really is. If open position is used, the heel of the advanced foot is placed directly forward on count one. On the next count it is brought directly in back of the other. Polka forward instead of to the side. The rest of the dance (turning) remains the same.

Many people confuse the Heel-and-Toe Polka with the Military Schottische, when the former is done in open position. Actually there is little resemblance between the two dances, except the open position.

The Poles, in particular, have adopted the Polka into their own rich assortment of national dances. If you would hear Polkas played at their best, listen to a good Polish orchestra some time. Better yet, go to the Polish National Home, on Governor Street in Hartford, Connecticut, any Tuesday night and see them danced in the proper atmosphere. You will come away with a high feeling of respect for Polish people and their customs, and more of an understanding of them than you ever had before. If you can't go, then by all means tune your radio to WTIC at 11:20 D.S.T. any Tuesday night.*

All Polkas are bouncy tunes, good for that tired-out feeling. In Polish orchestras, the biting staccato notes of cornet and clarinet dominate.

The original name by which the Polka was known was the Nimra. This name came from the song to which it was danced, the first three lines of which go something like this:

> *Strycek Nimra*
> *Koupil simla*
> *Za pul pata tolaru*

which translated into Yankee means:

> *Uncle Nimra*
> *Bought a white horse*
> *For five and one half thalers.*

Before leaving the subject of polkas we must tell you about the Polka Mazourka, another member of the prolific polka family. This dance is of Polish origin, and, a few years ago was found on every dance program. Then it was replaced by the Two-Step. It required a bit of patience to learn the Polka

* Which was the hour of the program at the time this book went to press.

1976 note: Polkas may no longer be danced every Tuesday at the Polish National Home, but Polka music is broadcast from Hartford faithfully still.

ourka, whereas the greenest beginner with ten
.nutes' practice could acceptably perform the Two-
Step.

POLKA MAZOURKA

Waltz Position   *Music in* 3/4 *Time*

The Polka Mazourka is a combination of the Polka
and Mazourka steps. Gent starts with left foot, lady
with right foot. Ladies' steps, of course, are the reverse of the gents' which are given below.

> Slide left foot to side, count 1
> Draw right foot to left, count 2
> Raise left foot to side, ankle high, toe pointed to the floor,
>   and at the same time raise and lower the heel of right
>   foot, count 3
> Slide left foot to left side, count 4
> Draw right foot to left, count 5
> Step back on left foot (turning), count 6
> Repeat everything, starting with the right foot and sliding
>   to the right. The entire dance is nothing more than this:
>   slide, close, raise, slide, close, step back. Slide, close, raise
>   (this time the right foot), slide, close, step forward.

The curious thing about the Polka-mania was that
it revived the other round dances which had not quite
taken hold, and inspired many new ones. Some of
these had butterfly duration, while others have lasted
until today. Predating the Polka was the Galop, which

LADIES GRAND CHAIN

(See page 39)

really needed the Polka craze to put it in the ascendency. In its early development the dance just lacked the "it" to put it across. Originally German and called the Hopser or Rutscher which described the step, the French took it over, renaming it the Galopade. In London it was shortened to the Galop, its present name. Webster will tell you to pronounce the word as spelled, but if you don't want to elicit Yankee scorn, call it what it is called hereabouts—*galow*.

Galops are still very popular in many parts of New England. We have been to dances when three or four would be played during the evening. True enough, not many of the young ones were doing the Galop. But they liked the tunes and slid enthusiastically about in some sort of an open-position fox trot, the boy's left hand joined with his partner's right, and held straight out in front like a bowsprit on a schooner.

Most of the Galops have an introduction and a coda, as well as one, and sometimes two, trios. Some of the most popular Galops are: Whip and Spur, Soho, Flip Flap and Blue Streak. Many orchestras will play one "legitimate" Galop, and an encore, and for the concluding number will play something like Red Wing, Jingle Bells, or Coming Round the Mountain. You see that "kitchen junket airs" are creeping into round dances too.

The dance itself is a spirited affair, sometimes turning into a ballroom marathon. It is done in 2/4 time and is extremely easy to learn.

GALOP

Waltz Position

Slide the left foot sideways, count 1

Bring the right foot up behind the heel of the left, count 2

Repeat this until a change of direction is wanted. To reverse the steps, repeat the same movement, sliding with the right foot first, sideways to the right. The lady performs the same steps as her partner, except that the feet are reversed.

Unlike the Galop, the once popular Schottische has today almost languished into disuse. It is said that probably the five-step variety, in which five steps were done in four counts, was responsible for its ultimate death. Forty years ago a dancer wasn't considered a finished product unless he could give a creditable performance of the Five-Step Schottische. But, as one old-time dancer puts it, the Five Step certainly finished many a good dancer.

The Schottische is of Polish extraction, and was introduced into this country shortly after the Polka. It was at first known as the German Polka, though the connection between the name and the Polish dance is somewhat vague. The music is very much like the Polka, but should be played slightly slower.

SCHOTTISCHE

Waltz Position. Music in 2/4 Time

Slide left foot to side, count 1
Close right foot to left, count 2
Slide left foot to side, count 3
Close right foot to left (raised, weight is still on left foot) and at the same time raise and lower the heel of the left foot, count 4
Repeat the same movements with the right foot to the right side
Second part
Execute 4 step hops turning, starting with left foot and alternating. Repeat all from the beginning.

Now, in case you want to try it, here is the Five Step. This Schottische variety is of New England birth, having been composed about 1870 by E. W. Masters of Boston, one of the best dancing instructors of his day:

FIVE-STEP SCHOTTISCHE

Waltz Position. Music in 2/4 Time

Slide left foot to left side, count 1
Draw right foot to left, count 2
Step back with left foot, turning, count 3

Slide right foot to right side, count *and*

Draw left foot to right, count 4. (The last two steps are really done to one full count, you see, making 5 steps to 4 counts.) Repeat with right foot like this:

Slide right foot to right side, count 1

Draw left foot to right, count 2

Step forward on right foot, count 3

Slide left foot to left side, count *and*

Draw right foot to left, count 4

Repeat all from the beginning. Remember to count the dance like this: 1, 2, 3 and 4. Turns are made the same as in a waltz.

The Two-Step completes the most favored of the dances of the Gay Nineties. This dance is still going strong in many parts of New England. Probably the national hunger for brass band marches is the secret of its success. Any march in 6/8 time is easily adaptable to a Two-Step. A list of such numbers is easily available, but they are too numerous to mention, as auction bills put it.

TWO-STEP

Waltz Position. Martial Music

Slide left foot to left side, count 1

Close right foot to left, and immediately step back on left foot, count *and* 2

Repeat the same with the right foot, using each foot alternately to commence the step. The lady's steps are the same as the gent's, except feet are reversed.

For the five dances that enjoyed lasting popularity, there are any number of dances of the past generation which went up like a rocket and came down like the stick. The names are legion. There was the Detroit, the Boston, the Berlin, the Veleta Waltz, the Newport, the Ripple, the Narragansett and the Duchess. The reason for their passing is that most of them originated, not with the common people of the soil, but in city ballrooms, where diversion and variety were sought for their own sake. Like the popular songs of today, most of them were intended to last only until a newcomer came along.

In passing, we might mention two more dances: the Gavotte and the Mazourka.

The Gavotte is a French dance which dates from the early part of the seventeenth century. It was then a dance of the Gavots, or people of the Gap, a department of the Upper Alps in France. At that time it was a peasant dance with steps and music very similar to the minuet.

A few generations of languid cultivation refined all the enthusiasm out of it. Marie Antoinette revived it for a time, but not until after the French Revolution did it obtain any widespread popularity. This interest was due chiefly to an opera dancer named Gardil, who made it over to suit himself, leaving out the little jumping steps which distinguished an earlier form.

The Mazourka is a horse of another color. This is a national Polish dance, getting its name from the early Palatinate of Marsovia. The dance dates back to the sixteenth century, and is still danced by the Polish people. It is noteworthy in that the dancers are allowed a lot of liberty in improvising new steps and figures. This makes it a difficult dance to follow. The time is ¾, though somewhat slower than an ordinary waltz.

Most of the dances which have just been described had their military counterparts—the Military Schottische, the Military Polka and the Military Two-Step. Henry Wilson used to call these military hotchas "the hop, skip and jumps," and generally they were known as the kicking dances.

The Military Schottische was also known as the Barn Dance, which title came from a popular tune called Dancing in the Barn. The tune which was most frequently played for it was the Rochester Schottische, one of the very first American-composed schottisches. The dance is divided into two parts.

MILITARY SCHOTTISCHE

MUSIC: Rochester Schottishe

First Part, Open Position

Partners stand side by side, gent's right hand at lady's waist, her left hand resting on his right arm. Each starts with left foot.

Take three short running steps forward, left, right, left, then hop on left foot, count 1, 2, 3, 4

Start with right foot and take three short running steps forward, right, left, right, then hop on right foot, count 5,
6, 7, 8

Second part is now done; waltz position making one-quarter
turn each time on each step.

Step back on left foot and hop, count 1, 2

Step forward on right foot and hop, count 3, 4

Step back on left foot and hop, count 5, 6

Step forward on right foot and hop, count 7, 8

Now begin with first part and repeat all from the beginning.

The dance is not nearly so complicated as it sounds.
The only difficult part is to dance it gracefully and
in perfect time with your partner, else there is considerable danger to your feet and peace of mind.

The Military Polka was also known as the Hornpipe Polka, because the first part of the tune is written in Hornpipe tempo. Incidentally, it is a swell
Hornpipe, and the way Arthur Maynard of Keene,
New Hampshire, plays it, with original grace notes
and variations, is worth going a long distance to hear.

MILITARY POLKA

MUSIC: Hornpipe Polka

Waltz Position

Lady commences with right foot. Gent with the left.

Two polka steps forward, counting 1, 2, 3 and 1, 2, 3

Two galop steps, counting 1, 2

Then polka steps, counting 1, 2, 3 and 1, 2, 3, and etc.

Continue the dance, alternating polka and galop steps.

The Military Two-Step, as described here, may or may not be done anywhere else in New England today besides our own town. All we know about it is that once a young Scot, a Commonwealth Fellow from St. Andrew's at Yale, introduced this dance at a ski-ball, and in no time at all the entire town hall rollicked with it. Now it is a part of our Saturday night programs. We call it:

GEORGE YOUNG'S MILITARY TWO-STEP

> FIRST PART: Partners in open position. Gent and lady start with outside foot
>
> Extend outside foot forward, heel on floor, toe raised, count 1, 2
>
> Bring outside foot back behind heel of the inside foot, toe on floor, heel raised, count 3, 4
>
> Walk forward 3 steps, turn on the fourth count and repeat all of above figures in opposite direction
>
> Partners then face each other, join right hands, make two short two-steps to the right, then back to the left
>
> Still holding hands, the lady pirouettes while the gent two-steps in place
>
> SECOND PART: Waltz position. Partners now two-step around hall for 8 measures. Then the whole figure is repeated from the beginning.

During the first part of the dance, the gents should carry themselves in their best soldierly style, as if they had sabers and rows of glittering medals to display. George Young had just that feeling for military pageantry (you should have heard him play the bagpipes; up and down the road he'd march, a solemn procession of one). A typical Scot, red hair and all, he gave that authentic air to the dance which inspired us all.

Just so must the dancers of the Seventies have been won over by the "different" air lent by the new round dances; for the popularity of the squares and contrys was seriously threatened for a while. But fortunately along came the "freaks and lace-trimmings" and applied the smelling salts, which was precisely what was needed to reinstate the expiring old-timers for life.

1976 note: 1870's, that is.

FREAKS AND FURBELOWS

Chapter X

Not long after the Polkas and their tribe threatened to squelch the country dances, somebody left a surprise basket on the door-step. The basket, it turned out, contained just the right formula to save the situation. Here were dances which so cleverly spliced the old and the new that the result was far more palatable than either. Here was just the right amount of freedom in the set figures. People fell for them so hard that it wasn't long before they forgot most of the numbers which had threatened death for the country dances back in the Sixties. Today few of us have more than heard of the Redowa and the Gorlitza.

All forward and back, pass on to the next was the magic call that satisfied the new ballroom wanderlust. Perhaps the "new" dances included a square dance call or two, or maybe a jig or reel motif, with the whole executed as a round dance. That's why we call them freaks!

Today's most favored freaks include the Sicilian Circle (often called the Portland Fancy), which we have already described, and the Soldier's Joy. This last is similar to the Circle and is very easy to do. It is supposed to have originated in Vermont. The original tune was written for an Irish Hornpipe, but it fitted this far different dance with equal success. The main theme, unchanged, was garnished with grace notes, triplets and syncopation according to the local fiddler's skill. Let's take a look at it and see what makes it go:

SOLDIER'S JOY

MUSIC: The Same

Dancers form in a circle around the hall as for Sicilian Circle: two couples in a set facing each other.

All forward and back	4 bars
Forward again and turn the opposite	4 "
All balance and turn partner	8 "
Ladies chain	8 "
Forward and back, pass on to the next	8 "

Repeat as long as desired, preferably stopping before any of the dancers faint or a fiddler's arm drops off.

We have referred to Portland Fancy several times, and this is how it used to be done around here:

PORTLAND FANCY

MUSIC: The Same

Form the Same as for Quadrille

First four right and left	8 bars
Same four promenade	8 "
Ladies chain	8 "
Same four promenade	8 "
Side couples repeat changes, then:	
First four lead to the right	4 "
Chassez out and form lines	4 "
(First four give both hands to opposite and turn three-quarters round to right.)	
All forward and back	4 "
Ladies cross over to partners	4 "

The prompter now stops the music and says "Form lines for Portland Fancy." The music starts and:

Eight hands around	8 "
Right and left	8 "
Ladies chain	8 "
All forward and back, pass on to next	8 "

Repeat the second part several times before ending the dance.

Another of these frolicsome affairs was the Down-east Breakdown, usually danced to the tune of Thunder Hornpipe, though not always, for the Rout, and Flowers of Edinburgh were sometimes played for it.

DOWNEAST BREAKDOWN

MUSIC: Thunder Hornpipe or The Rout

Form as for the Circle except that each set is composed of four couples, two couples standing side by side, facing two other couples also standing side by side.

Eight hands around	8 bars
Right and left	8 "
Ladies chain	8 "
Forward and back, pass on to the next	8 "

In this last change, the couples that are going around the hall to the left, join hands and raise them over their heads, while the couples progressing to the right, stoop and pass through. Each two couples remain together throughout the dance.

Another one just freaky enough to keep you on your toes is the California Reel. The reason for the name is unknown, but it is an all-fired good number if you keep your wits about you. Here is one way of doing it:

CALIFORNIA REEL

MUSIC: Devil's Dream, the second strain of which is played through three times instead of the usual twice.

Form as for the Downeast Breakdown

Eight hands around	8 bars
Outside couples balance and swing	8 "
(Inside couples right and left at same time.)	
Outside couples right and left	8 "
(Inside couples balance and swing at same time.)	
Ladies chain	8 "
All forward and back, pass on to the next	8 "

POP GOES THE WEASEL

(See page 94)

SCOTCH REEL

MUSIC: Come Under My Plaidie. The second strain must be played three times.

Form as for Sicilian Circle

Turn the opposite with right hand	4 bars
Turn partner with left hand	4 "
Promenade four	8 "
Ladies chain	8 "
Right and left	8 "
Forward and back, pass on to the next	8 "

Continue as long as desired.

Swedish immigrants are responsible for the introduction of the following number. In any gathering where there is a man-shortage, this dance is deservedly well-liked, for each man takes care of two partners, one on either side of him. Well we remember the Big Swede in our town (he had a name but nobody ever called him by it) as he used to stride out to dance with two dames. A grin cut his face in two and his blonde head sat perfectly erect on his huge body, as if he were entertaining an imaginary carbuncle on the back of his neck.

SWEDISH DANCE

MUSIC: *Buffalo Gals*

Form in a circle around the hall as in Sicilian Circle, three dancers are facing three others, the gent in the middle.

All join hands forward and back twice	8 bars
Each gent balance and swing opposite lady on his right	8 "
Balance and swing opposite left hand lady	8 "
Each gent back to place, forward and back, forward again, pass on to the next	8 "

Second Part

All forward and back twice	8 "
Top ladies (the ones on outside) and opposite gent three hands around	8 "
Other two ladies and gent three hands around	8 "
(The call is three hands around, but each trio circle several times around.)	
All forward and back, forward again, pass on to the next	8 "

Third Part

All forward and back twice	8	bars
Four ladies cross right hands half round	4	"
Left hands back to place	4	"
Six hands around	8	"
All forward and back, forward again, pass on to the next	8	"

All these figures are now repeated, and so on until the prompter ends the dance or some poor hapless man, not quite so Swedish in stamina, faints of exhaustion.

Undoubtedly the freakiest of all the freaks is the renowned Spanish Dance. Only postgraduates of the Downeast ballet should try this. Freshmen should just sit quietly by and watch. This dance is something to see, all stepped out to slow waltz time.

SPANISH DANCE

MUSIC: The Same

Form as for the Circle

Forward four	2	bars
Change partners	2	"
Forward four	2	"
Change partners	2	"

Forward four	2	bars
Change partners	2	"
Forward four	2	"
Change partners	2	"
Cross right hands half around	4	"
Left hands back to place	4	"
All waltz	8	"

Repeat above calls as long as desired.

Now, lest this look like a typesetter's orgy, here is a more detailed explanation. Remember, everything is done in slow waltz time.

Forward four. Each gent takes partner's left hand in his right; forward one step, raising joined hands in front. One step back again, lowering hands.

Change partners. Couples forward one step as before, the gents remain, the ladies cross over, placing left hands in opposite gent's right. The new partners turn part way round so as to occupy a position at right angles to first position.

Forward four and change partners. Same as above, repeated, bringing partners together again, but occupying opposite positions to their original one.

Forward four and change partners. Balance again and change partners as before, being now at left angles to first position.

Forward four and change partners. Same as before, you are now back in your original position beside partner.

Cross right hands half around has already been described.

All waltz. Each couple waltzes around its own set or square once and a half times, stopping a new couple and repeating the same figures.

Now in case you still think that Yankee farmers are gauche on the dance floor, watch this done, not only as above, but as a double dance, with four couples to a set instead of two! The best of dancers do it that way. Enough of this. The description is even going to our heads.

Did you ever know a fireman to be left out of anything hot and exciting? This next dance may or may not have been originated by some hook-and-ladder company, but it was always played at firemen's balls, and was as much a part of all smoke-eaters' lives as their red suspenders.

FIREMAN'S DANCE

MUSIC: *Flannel Jacket*, the second strain of which is played through three times instead of the usual twice.

Dancers form as for the Downeast Breakdown. Before starting the dance the prompter should advise which couples are "Here" and which are "There." As a usual thing the couples on the inside are called "There" and the couples on the outside are called "Here."

Outside here, inside there   **8 bars**
> (Couples "Here" cross hands, chassez eight steps toward the inside and return to place. At the same time couples called "There" chassez eight steps in opposite direction and return to place, separating each time to let the other couples pass through.)

Inside here, outside there   8 bars
   (Reverse the above movement.)
Ladies chain here, right and left there   8 "
Right and left here, ladies chain there   8 "
Forward and back, pass on to the next   8 "
Continue as long as desired.

Few people now living can remember the fancy contrys. The dances didn't survive, which is not surprising, for nothing fancy ever does. But in their day, like those burnt-wood handkerchief boxes and gilded cat-tails which gathered dust in the corner of the front room, they were quite something.

Imagine a polka or waltz in contry formation! Especially in favor in the more sophisticated ballrooms of New England, they were once necessities on every formal dance program. We are indebted to England for a few of them, but the great majority are as American as pumpkin pie.

No music score was too hallowed, no composer too noted to escape. As far as can be learned, every one of these graduate dances originated with band or dancing masters. The zenith of their popularity (the dances, not the masters) was reached in the eighteen sixties and seventies, although they did not die out completely until much later.

One of the best known was the Jenny Lind Polka. The dedication is obvious and fitting, for was not everything from a bird cage bustle to a nickel cigar named after the Swedish songbird?

JENNY LIND POLKA

MUSIC: *The Same*

Form as for Contry Dance

First two couples balance and turn	8 bars
Same two couples polka down the center	4 "
First couple up the outside, ladies' side. Second couple up the other side at same time	4 "
Same two couples cross right hands half around	4 "
Left hands back to place	4 "
Half promenade	4 "
Half right and left	4 "

The head couple now goes below one couple and repeats the figure with the third couple and so on. After one repetition the second couple starts, etc.

One of England's dancing masters, Mr. Layland of London was the author of the following Polka Contry which became the talk of this country soon after its introduction here.

POLKA CONTRY

MUSIC: *Any Heel and Toe Polka*

Form as for Contry Dance, two lines facing each other. Couples stand side by side, in open position.

All balance partner twice, polka across the set, couples passing to right of each other	8 bars

All balance twice and polka back to place	8 bars
All ladies chain	8 "
Two head couples polka around each other	8 "
Same two couples polka down the center and take places at the foot of the set	8 "

Repeat until all have done the changes. All polka for remainder of the dance.

Hohnstock's, Sultan, Cologne and Baden-Baden Polka Contrys all had their followers in their heyday. Hohnstock's especially, was played and danced by every up and coming group throughout New England.

Along with the later Waltz Quadrilles came the Waltz Contrys—The Cinderella, Spanish, Hungarian, German and Silver Lake. This last bears a decided resemblance to the jig, Twin Sisters, previously mentioned.

SILVER LAKE WALTZ

MUSIC: The Same

Form Regular Contry Lineup . . . Six or Eight Couples in a Set

First and second ladies join hands and waltz across the set and back	8 bars
First and second gents waltz across and back at the same time, passing on outside of ladies.	
First and second gents join hands and waltz across the set and back	8 "
First and second ladies waltz across and back at the same time. Passing on outside of gents.	

First couple waltz around each other and back to
place below one couple   **8 bars**

Repeat until all are back in their original positions.
Then all waltz remainder of the dance. After one
repetition of the changes the second couple starts
and follows the first down the line, etc.

The Magnolia Waltz, later called the Steamboat Waltz, was well known on all the larger side-
wheelers. In fact it was started on a river boat, the
steps having been worked out by one Robert Layden
(of the Rhode Island Laydens) when he was not in
conference over a gambling table.

STEAMBOAT WALTZ

MUSIC: The Same

Form as for Regular Contry Dance. Six or Eight Couples in a Set

First couple join hands and waltz down the outside,
ladies side   8 bars
Second couple waltz down the center at same time.
First couple waltz up the center   8 "
Second couple waltz up the outside, gents' side at
same time.
First two couples balance, half right and left 8 "
Balance again, waltz around each other to place 8 "

Repeat until all have done the figure. Then all waltz
while the music is played once through the tune.

Completing these contry freaks is the Holly Berry, once called a "Country Dance For All Times." It enjoyed a brief whirl for about a half a dozen years and then faded. Such are our prophets!

THE HOLLY BERRY

MUSIC: Any Galop

Regular Contry Lance Line-up . . *Six or Eight Couples in a Set*

All forward and back	4 bars
All cross over	4 "
Every two couples give right hands half around	4 "
Left hands back	4 "
Head couple galop down the center and cross right hands half around with foot couple	4 "
Head and foot couples left hands back	4 "

Two top couples also cross hands half around at same time.

The couple that is now at the head, galop round the room followed in line by the rest of the set, until they come back to the places they just left. Then, lining up in contry dance formation again, they repeat the changes until all have reached their starting positions. The dance then ends.

All of these side-show dances were done in the bustle era. Your mother remembers them, and remembers when every skirt had a plackett, that small opening at the back of a skirt, fastened with hooks and eyes.

Attending a dance at Stoddard, New Hampshire, some sixty odd years ago, was a very proud lady who, in order to keep her bustle in place, had tied to it as ballast a small bag filled with sawdust.

Unfortunately one of the plackett fasteners came unhooked, and a certain village prankster happened by and noticed a golden opportunity. Taking out his jack knife, he opened the small blade and prepared to make a neat little incision in the bag.

Soon, of course, things were happening. Sawdust geysered forth at every whirl. Funny to all the dancers, yes. But imagine the poor woman's embarrassment when she discovered that her prized possession had deflated and shifted its course! And right in public, my dear!

1976 note: If your mother doesn't recall these things, perhaps your grandmother will.

PROMENADE FOUR
(See page 40)

WHO'S WHO
NOW AND THEN

WHEREIN ARE DESCRIBED THE DEVIL'S

DREAMERS, PIGEON'S WINGERS & ROAR-

ING BULLS OF YESTERDAY & TODAY

Chapter XI

In picking out the fine fiddlers and fiddle makers, the dancing masters, the dancers and the callers of today, yesterday and the days before, you must remember that we are merely choosing the bright-colored bits from our own private scrapbag. Heaven knows New England has many, many more of these grand individuals to offer; but, as throughout this book, we are depending only upon our own experience. We only hope that these exclusions will inspire you to remember those you had all but forgotten.

Fiddle makers are rare, and good fiddle makers, rarer. When we were down in Frankfort, Maine, (they say that if you address a letter to "Minkhole, Maine," it would go straight as an arrow to the Frankfort Post Office) we paid a visit to the village smithy. Alvah Batchelder, the blacksmith, is also a maker of violins. He is one of the best that New England has ever produced; and because he is in the top brackets he doesn't make things by the yard for the trade. No, indeed. He has made only fifty-five violins and three violas in his life.

His father was a violin maker before him, so the talent runs in the blood. When we were there Alvah had two backs glued together ready for sawing into a rough outline preparatory to carving into shape. One was a magnificent flaming maple and the other was butterfly maple with extremely wide grain that looked almost as if it were fluted; but when we passed our hand over it, it felt as smooth as a school ma'am's leg. When Alvah touched these violin backs you felt his very fingers could visualize the finished instrument.

Selling his creations is not in the least Mr. Batchelder's concern. But since his fiddles are such extraordinary specimens, they automatically sell themselves. And since he became duly recognized as a master workman, members of the Boston Symphony Orchestra have been bringing their highly insured stringed instruments to him for repairs.

"Course, some fellers buy the backs and tops already for graduating, from the big music houses, you know," Batchelder explained, "but I never have. I like to know the story of every piece of wood I use ... except for the ebony finger-board and pegs, that is. Now, this violin here is made of wood that came off this very place of mine."

He handed us a violin, and a few minutes of playing on it convinced us that here was something to be cherished.

"Seventy-five dollars," said Batchelder in reply to our inquiry about price. "But it ain't quite ready yet. Needs another coat of varnish. That other one now ... I don't want to sell that just yet. Kind of like to play on it myself."

And Alvah played. Shades of Mellie Dunham, could he play! None of this first and last note and one or two in the middle business; but every note, clear as cellophane. Did he know any of Ross' reels? Yes, sir. All five of them. And a sixth one that he had composed himself. With his daughter at the piano and his son stroking a bull fiddle, he played for an hour. And never before have sixty minutes passed so quickly.

Laying aside his violin as abruptly as he had taken it up, Mr. Batchelder said simply: "My next violin will have a good, full G and D, a mellow A and a brilliant E. That's putting it pretty strong, now ain't it? But I know I can do it."

We went over to Mrs. Quigley's house then. She is a woman of seventy odd, and spry. We wanted to know what the most favored dances of that neighborhood have been. Hull's Victory, Money Musk and Boston Fancy, it seemed. Over strong Irish tea, she reminisced about the stern old dancing days of her youth. The dancing masters, she said, spent a lot of time grilling the young people in the P's and Q's of the ballroom. One of these, Alvin Yorke, would brook no hilarity among his pupils. One evening he spied a gangling country boy flapping his arms about and otherwise abandoning himself to the spell of the fiddle. Stopping the music, Yorke pointed a long finger of scorn at the kid, called his name, and said: "We will have no more of this outrageous nonsense. This is a dancing school, not a kitchen sweat."

Our visit to Minkhole inspired us to do something about getting a better fiddle for ourselves. Since we couldn't afford a Batchelder at that time, we went over to Peterborough to see what Forrest Barrett had to swap. An old-time fiddler of state-wide renown, Barrett has for years quietly carried on his hobby of violin trading. "A lot of folks think I get the best of every trade, but I don't. Sometimes I make a little money on one, and perhaps lose it all and more with it on the next one," Mr. Barrett told us.

At the time we visited him, Mr. Barrett had fifteen violins, all of them strung up and waiting to be traded. It seemed that a story hovered over every one of them. "That dark colored one I got from a young man living nearby. Pretty good fiddle player, too. He went to war and traveled around over there quite a bit afterwards. Happened that one day he was in Vienna, Austria, and bought this violin from an old man there in the city. No, he didn't say it was a pawn shop; might have been, but I don't think so. Well, a few years ago, the young fellow had to go out west for his health, and that was how I got it. He's dead now. Poison gas, you know."

One of Barrett's fiddles was once swapped by an Irishman for a side of pork. Another was bought at a country auction for less than three dollars and served a young man's apprenticeship until he could afford something a little better.

Mr. Barrett scoffs at the idea that the dance Wild Goose Chase was so named by Federal soldiers floundering vainly after Jeb Stuart. "Why, old Sewall Page has told me about playing that tune a good many years before the Civil War. Called it Wild Goose Chase, too. Goes something like this . . ." and after one or two flourishes of the bow, he played it for us. First a simple, direct melody, and then a bow-twisting variation, probably his own, although he didn't say so.

"Here's another good old tune," he went on, and giving the patented E string adjuster a minute turn to the right, he swept into Chorus Jig as we never expect to hear it played again.

WILD GOOSE CHASE

(*As recorded by Forrest Barrett*)

"I know you'll like that violin," he said to us. "It's new, but it has an improvin' tone. I'll be sure to write off that Wild Goose Chase and bring it up sometime . . . you know," he said, as we were leaving, "I sometimes wish that all the old fiddlers and prompters could belong to a club and have meetings every now and then. Seems as though somebody ought to start one." At that time we did not know of Edward Rand of Warner, New Hampshire, who has done that very thing.

Edward Rand is a fiddler of more than local renown. Eighty-one years old and looking not a minute over sixty, he still plays for dances in and about his home town. His trading stock of fiddles is worth seeing, also. When we were there he had over thirty, all of them strung up and ready to play.

In 1936 Mr. Rand conceived a Fiddlers' Old Home Day. Fourteen old fiddlers came to his place for this first meeting to fiddle and reminisce. We hope that this becomes a permanent feature somewhere in New England every year.

And we'd like to see an Old Home Day for

1976 note: Fiddlers both young and old do indeed foregather in many corners of the land for an annual jamboree.

prompters, too. Of course, it would probably be a monkey house for noise! All prompters have so much to say, on or off the platform. We're glad we didn't have to gather Wallace Dunn's ideas, for instance, amidst loud competition from a score of other prompters. He just sat quietly in his parlor and told us what he thought of the prompters of today.

"The trouble with most prompters now'days," he said, "is they don't know when to call. They are just as apt to holler 'Down the Center' right in the middle of a measure as they are to vote straight Republican." Wallace Dunn ought to know what he's talking about, for thirty years ago he was considered about tops. And tops in those days was topper than tops: it was not uncommon to have six or seven quadrilles on an evening's program, you know; and Mr. Dunn was able to call that many, each five-figured, without repeating a call!

"The time to call," went on Mr. Dunn, "is just before the end of a measure, so that the dancers will get it just as the strain begins. That's where the call belongs. Another reason a lot of prompters get mixed up is because they follow the dancers, and there ain't one dancer in a hundred now'days that will keep time to the music, let alone knowing how many beats it takes to do right and left. A prompter who knows his business will do the leading, and a good dancer will do the following. You see what I mean?"

Mr. Dunn first began calling at some of the impromptu kitchen dances near his home in Munsonville, New Hampshire. Word soon got bruited about that here was a young fellow who knew his business, and it wasn't long before he was in constant demand. Many a time, he says, he got home from a dance with just time enough to change his clothes and hitch up the four-horse team that he drove for the L. J. Colony Chair Company.

Wallace Dunn was no second-rater on the fiddle, either, but he was content to play second and call with the orchestra at the same time.

Whenever a group became a bit conceited and demanded more complicated calls for their quadrilles, Mr. Dunn usually obliged with the following:

> *First four lead to the right*
> *Chassez out and form a line*
> *The ladies chain in line*
> *Chain across*
> *Chain in line*
> *Chain across*
> *Turn partners, and all promenade*

It isn't every amateur dancer who can do the Dunn combination. As we said before in our chapter on quadrilles, in most groups there is ever an unspoken challenge to the prompter to try to confuse the dancers who seem to know the simple calls too well.

"About the hardest thing a caller has to contend with now'days," continued Mr. Dunn, "is the orchestra itself. When I first begun to call, we had two violins, a cornet, clarinet and bass viol. You can't beat that combination for contry dances. Now'days they have too much brass, and everyone tries to drown out the other fellow.

"A few years ago we had dances here in Munsonville. Had an orchestra up from Massachusetts, pretty good too, except I thought they played Irish Washerwoman too much. Well, their prompter wanted to dance a quadrille and asked me to call it for him. Got along all right enough 'til all of a sudden there was an awful crash-bang right behind me. Lord, I thought the stovepipe had fell down, but it was only the drummer with some of his clap-trap. *We* never needed that stuff to keep time to the music, but maybe they do now'days."

Of course, dances vary more now than they did in the old days. Some orchestras may play "clap-trap," while others may be much more quiet. Some may feature nearly all contrys, while others prefer most all squares. At Charlemont, Massachusetts, the program of the evening seemed to be two quadrilles and a contry, two quadrilles and a contry, and so on through the night. Oh, there were two or three waltzes and a couple of two-steps spliced in before the night was over, but you could have called it a *square* dance and been pretty nearly right. The hall was full; the crowd was mainly young. Didn't they want any modern dances? If they did, they were quieter about it than any other group of youngsters we ever saw. At the finish of a quadrille they stayed right on the floor, taking their rest on their feet. Does that look like they favored modern slinkabouts?

Harry Shippee got us down there. He's one of those grand old men, now over eighty, who has played for dances since he was in knee pants. Only a few years ago he played for over two hundred dances in a year's time; and that didn't count lots of private shindigs, either.

"Used to go round quite a lot to rich folks' houses and play all evenin' for them. No, they didn't dance . . . just set round listenin' to the music and gettin' me to tell about old times.

"The young people now'days," Shippee went on, "want their music played faster than it was when I first begun playin'. They want dances with a lot of swingin' in 'em, too, and not much balancin'. Look at 'em out there. Ain't they havin' a grand time?" Carelessly he tucked his fiddle under his chin and joined in with Money Musk.

The prompter here was a young French-Canadian, Ambrose LaNue (see chapter on quadrilles). He had grown up with Shippee's orchestra and had naturally fallen into the art of prompting. "The best caller in the New England states," Shippee introduced him to us. That, of course, is Mr. Shippee's opinion; but he certainly knows as many changes as anybody else, and some that only a few know. He obligingly called his "Dive for oysters, dive for clams, dive for home in the Promised Land." It was a lot of fun.

"The best caller" . . . "the best fiddler" . . . those are phrases that have rung down the years. Much is based on personal opinion, of course. Still, no one can deny that the "best" are always extra good. Take old Charlie Cavender, for instance. He was considered "the best" in our grandfathers' day. He lived over in Peterborough, New Hampshire, and was a blacksmith by trade. Why smithing and fiddling go together, we don't know; but it seems to be the ideal combination. Cavender couldn't read a note of music, but his ear was as sensitive as a safe-cracker's fingertips. When he was a young kid, he was busily taken up one evening with filling his mother's woodbox, when all of a sudden a tune he had been trying to remember, came to him. He dropped his armful of wood and tore for his fiddle to record the tune forever. People in Cheshire and Hillsborough counties still speak wonderingly of Cavender's ability to play for a dance until he fell asleep in his chair.

Individualism was as common among Yankee fiddlers as it was among Yankees in any other calling. Old Baker Moore, for example, firmly believed to his dying hour that on two separate occasions when playing for a dance, he had been "honored" with the personal assistance of the Devil. Moore, at that time was considered the best fiddler in Hillsborough county, New Hampshire, and noted for his improvisations on familiar dance tunes.

And there was Sewall Page, another star of his day. His neighbors, young and old, loved to drop in of an evening and just listen to Page for hours. The violin was part of his very life, and Page asked but two things of his guests: absolute silence, and no moving from the exact spots he designated as their places. He was all done for an evening, though, if a cat so much as walked across the floor. The relationship of catgut to the instrument he was playing was evidently not appreciated by him!

Of course, if Page had been blind like Old Blind Rice or Blind Dunbar, cats wouldn't have mattered. These two itinerant fiddlers drifted all over New England. Whenever one of them landed in our town he usually stayed a week . . . the farmers were always delighted to put him up. He would play, then, every evening for dancing or what we now call community singing. All present would toss appreciative coins in his hat.

It seems as if we've done nothing but talk about old fiddlers. That's quite a mistake. There are plenty of swell young musicians all around New England as you, yourself, can verify by making a tour of some of the country dances. You'll be surprised at the number there are, and more surprised at their ability.

Most of them, of course, grew right up with the contrys and squares and could have told the difference between Devil's Dream and Money Musk most before they were out of diapers. We, personally, know quite a few of these fellows, so suspect that each corner of the states has its crop of players who will keep up the tradition.

Carl Stewartson of Concord, New Hampshire, is one of them. He comes from a family of musicians that has not for generations produced an unmusical member. Carl is known as a promising young violinist throughout southern New Hampshire and northern Massachusetts. He inherited his passion for old-time contrys and acquired his technique from listening to his Uncle Leon Stewartson.

Young Wilfred Bonenfant of Suncook, New Hampshire, also grew up in the midst of old-time music. This young lad has the soul of a real fiddler. You know, some people play with the mechanical precision of a windshield wiper, and with about as much feeling. And others play technically as well, but with such a degree of artistry that their improvisations and personal expressions can be the despair of anyone trying to write down that particular version. We doubt if Bunny has ever played a tune the same way on two consecutive Saturday nights. Just *watching* him play . . . say you were deaf and couldn't hear a note . . . would make you want to dance. He has such a wonderful time playing that his joy is easily projected all through the dance hall. That, of course, is the essence of a real fiddler, be he eighty or just twenty-three.

Or even just "middle age" (whatever that may mean). Albert Quigley of Nelson, New Hampshire, is just between young and old. He is the son of the Mrs. Quigley of Minkhole with whom we shared that cup of reminiscent tea. Quig has played for dances since he was a barefoot boy. His father had a local orchestra, and Quig says he "can't remember

when Saturday didn't mean hog-wrastle night to me."
With the exception of Arthur Maynard of Keene,
New Hampshire, we believe no one in Cheshire
county can approach Quig's ability at jigging and
reeling. Quig is another true fiddler, able and willing
to extemporize on a tune. He also is an excellent
example of the versatility of many of our musicians.
No, he is not the village blacksmith (although he
could easily be—he is built like a bison, and we've
never seen anything he couldn't make with his
hands). As knitting work he will turn out a fine fiddle, but more important, he is rapidly becoming
recognized as a remarkable landscape painter, and his
hand-carved picture frames are the envy and despair
of imitators. He also can tell a story about as palatably
as anyone we've ever heard. Of course, we don't mention Quig's original music.

Arthur Maynard of Keene deserves recognition in
any assembly of great fiddlers. Mr. Maynard learned
the old dances from his father, and he claims he
knows every jig, reel or hornpipe ever published. No
one has come along to dispute this. Maynard is known
as an exceptionally "strong" player, and his friends
boast that, no matter what the size of the orchestra,
he has never yet been drowned out.

No round-up of fiddlers would be the real McCoy
if it did not include some mention of that grand old
man with the bow: Cassius Radford, of Concord, New
Hampshire. Back in 1926 when Cash was a young
man of seventy-nine, he won the state fiddling cham-

pionship, and then went on to take the New England crown and make a successful vaudeville tour.

And when speaking of vaudeville, we invariably think of Malcolm Hall's orchestra which hailed from Orange, Massachusetts. There were individuals in that outfit who were so good that they have since been grabbed up by vaudeville and the radio. Hall's accordion player . . . whatever *was* his name . . . lasted only a few months with us here in Nelson before he was offered a radio contract and booked as The Homesick Player of the Air or something like that. And Malcolm Hall, himself, is someone you'll hear of. He is simply a wonder of a pianist. Not only does he play every little jig-saw piece of every tune (an accomplishment in itself), but on top of that he improvises the most wonderful jazz figures you ever heard! We used to sit with our backs to the piano to get the full effect through our whole bodies. Ross Hornbeck, too, used to play every note of every country dance on the xylophone. It really makes us quite sad to see groups like this one bust up.

On the other hand, we get a big kick out of groups which will probably never go professional, like the Webster people. Calling themselves the Merrimack Merrymakers, these six couples from Webster, New Hampshire, are: Mr. and Mrs. Eugene Colby, Mr. and Mrs. Emerson Hoar, Mr. and Mrs. Gaylord Emery, Frank Keaton, Genevieve Bowers, Theda Stone, Ned Bowers, Sherman Stevens and Mrs. Katherine Phelps.

These people have been organized for several years as an old-fashioned dance group and have taken part in amateur tournament and outdoor festivities with a great deal of success. All of the group live in Webster or Boscawen and are under the direction of Mr. Ernest Downes, prompter and one of the last of the old-time dancing masters.

The ladies in this group wear beautiful gowns, replicas of those worn many years ago. The men wear striped trousers and cutaways, with flowing ties and dickies. The group is an ideal combination of young and old, which is so natural and normal to country dancing.

These people claim that they never rehearse before any of their performances, but there's a twinkle in their eyes when they tell you, daring you to be sucker enough to believe it!

Obviously, hats should come off to Mr. Downes. A very genial man, his weather-beaten face crinkles into a smile at the mention of old-time dances—they are his life. He doesn't know one note of music from another, and plays no musical instrument by ear, yet he has a perfect sense of rhythm, and besides, a great gift for teaching.

The particular "set piece" of this group is the best thing we've ever seen done to music. It's called the Combination Dance, and is original with Mr. Downes. It is far too puzzling to learn from print, but suffice it to say that it combines Hull's Victory and one version of Old Zip Coon. The first two

couples start the dance by doing Old Zip, the third
and fourth, Hull's Victory, and the fifth and sixth,
Old Zip. Everybody is dancing at the same time.
They change steps every other time, you see, doing
first Hull's Victory and then Old Zip. To end the
dance everybody does a few steps of a glide waltz.

This dance, like all real estate, should be seen to
be appreciated. We were lucky enough to see them
do it two separate times—and both times without
benefit of prompter! If Ernest Downes was shooting
them signals, the signals were expertly camouflaged.
We rather believe that the dancers were on their own.

Exhibit groups are grand fun to watch, but sometimes an extemporaneous bunch offers as much.

You should have popped in with us on Grange 518
in Ascutneyville, Vermont. The minute you parked
your car alongside the other Fords and Chevvies and
heard the full-bodied music coming through the open
windows, you would have suspected that here was no
"revival," no carrying on of a tradition in noble self-
consciousness. When you paid your quarter to the big
red-headed chap and walked onto the floor, you
would have known for sure.

The hall was well filled, and everyone was dancing. Who could have helped it—the orchestra would
have made a paralytic get up and turn a cart-wheel.
Every dancer was under thirty, it seemed, and, we
venture to guess, had never seen a city bigger than
Rutland. The orchestra was young, too, with the exception of one chap who looked fortyish, a music

teacher in the Springfield, Vermont, high school. It was a four piece orchestra, although the variety and volume made it sound like eight. There was a drummer who laid a perfect foundation for the others, a fiddler who also handled a saxophone and clarinet with skill, the music teacher who showed his versatility by switching from the banjo to the silver flute and piccolo, and Sidney Young, for whom the orchestra is named (and rightly), who managed an accordion so well that even Major Bowes would have said "All right, all right."

The caller, one Dennis Allen, was as good in his way as the orchestra. A big chap built on the lines of a WPA project, just twenty-four years old, he has a roar much like the noise that ice gives out when the temperature is falling fast. He has plenty of personality and a gift for holding things together. And beside all this, he sings his calls.

The dancers—all young, as we have said—were what might be called a "mixed" group. From what we could gather, there seemed to be a good representation of Poles, Irish, Finns, and Canucks, as well as Yankees. We thought the hall was well filled, but Allen told us that most everybody was at the Hartland Fair where they expected to win a bee-you-tiful new sedan with their door ticket. "You should come back next Friday."

Such dancing! You didn't have to be very bright to know that these people *had* to dance—that they needed to dance. The rhythm and originality of step came solely from that need. There was no feeling of "oh hell, here it is Friday night; we've got to go to the dance again." Here was no need for drinking, which is something quite out of the ordinary these days.

Every third dance was a country dance, but there was something about even the fox trots that reminded us of a quadrille or contry. For instance, there was the little French-Canadian chap who showed us a thing or two in the whirling line. We had complimented him on his ability to whirl, and then he told us that *that* was nothing—we should have seen him at Croyden, at the country dance contest last month! Whirl? Whew! He whirled his woman fourteen minutes, forty revolutions to the minute! Got a prize, too. Just to prove it, he grabbed the girl in the red blouse, and, to the tune of a fox trot just out, he spun her in that country dance half-step whirl all around the hall! Not once, but three times! As they progressed in this amazing performance, we felt as if we were watching a human illustration of the workings of the solar system.

Although we did a Hull's Victory (slightly different in one call) and a Soldier's Joy, most of the country dances were quadrilles. The one that got us was the Doodar, something we always wanted to see in the flesh. It went (something) like this:

DOODAR

To the tune of De Camptown Races

The head lady turn the right hand gent
  Once around, once around.

Back to your honey and left hand round
  Oh doodar day.
The lady in the center and seven hands around,
  The old red hen, the old red hen,
The hen flies out and the crow hops in
  Join your hands and around again
With your right foot up and your left foot down
  Keep with the music and shake 'er down.
Right and left your corners all
  And don't forget the other way
All balance your corners and mind what I say
  Swing your honey all way round, and
        promenade the same.

That was Vermont. Now we wanted to go in the other direction and see something way down the line; so we went to the Eastern States Exposition at Springfield, Massachusetts, one fall. We had always associated satin cattle with polished horns, or the latest in Diesel tractors, with fairs, but not country dance exhibits. But, as you probably know, there isn't anything that the Eastern States Exposition doesn't have.

Thanks to Mrs. Storrow, the exhibit was held in a large barn in her model New England town, Storrowton, where there is dancing every Friday night all summer. On each day of the fair, as we understood it, there was to be a different orchestra, caller and set of dancers. Luckily we went on Happy Hale's day.

Happy Hale is someone we'd been hearing about for years—a legend, almost, wherever you go. (He told us, with neither conceit nor modesty, "I'm a well-known figure from Maine to California.") We had visualized him as you do a legendary figure—an old guy with thinning white hair, who perhaps would have to sit down to call the last three dances. But imagine our surprise when this veteran of thirty years' prompting turned out to look as if that year might be his first chance to vote for President! (We even examined him in the strong sunlight that was streaming in through the wide-open barn doors and still we didn't change our first impressions.) There he stood, dressed in white with a bunch of cellophane-wrapped cigars bulging out of his polo shirt pocket. Just to look at him, built on the lines of a featherweight, you knew he could dance like a fool. When he finally got down from the platform and danced a Coming Through the Rye—oh well.

The orchestra was a trio consisting of fiddler, saxophone player (none of your over-ripe jazz saxophonists), and a pianist, one Louis Delude, who has been blind since he was six months old. Not a full orchestra, perhaps, but one which kept perfect time and played the jigs with both precision and imagination.

The dancers made up two sets of eight for quadrilles and an adequate line for the contrys. These were perfectly average looking people of mostly oldish years, fat and thin, tall and squat—the kind you can pick up by the handful at any typical country dance. Like the barn and surroundings, there was no introduction of professional quaintness, no feeling of exploitation. It was just a neighborly group, getting together for a whirl. It would be hard to describe how good these people were. We have seen just as fine dancing in our town, to be sure; but not so consistently fine. This must, of course, have been a culled group which was used to dancing together. When they did Hull's Victory, for instance, the *tum tee tum tum— tum, tum, tum*—you know the strain that runs all through it—was tapped out in one universal tap figure. This step, while it appeared to be uniform, was made up of steps as individual to each dancer as his own thumb print. That, we think, symbolizes all country dancing: the spirit of the whole first, the individual next.

Now to get back to Happy Hale. He is one of those callers who make history. He keeps the dances going with a thousand little "fill-in" calls which he has available.

Hale told us that he was thinking of giving up calling—no money in it any more. "You know," he said, "I don't sit down on the job like lots of callers. I give 'em a full evening's worth, calling all the time. We have the orchestra tuned to B flat, and I can go on forever in that key. Other keys are either too high or too low for me, and I get hoarse and can't keep going every minute."

While we understood Happy Hale's point of view, we felt that it would be a crime if he were to give up calling. You could tell that he really loved it.

Since that fall we have had Happy Hale in our town every Saturday night. Of course, we are still frogs hollering for our own puddle, remember, but we think that Hale is the finest caller in the country. We have heard a fair representation, but Hale seems to be head and shoulders above the best. You probably have your favorite, too, but don't button up your conclusion for good until you have studied the requirements for a good caller and have danced at least once under Hale's leadership.

A good caller must have a simon-pure sense of rhythm and an excellent ear for music. He must have a pleasing personality and a sympathetic understanding of a beginner's troubles. He must have the talent of keeping cheerful under all circumstances, even when he is inwardly disgusted with a dance group and is dying to cuss them out; in other words, he must be able to smile "when all about him . . ." Of course, he must be a good teacher, for nowadays, with no dancing masters floating about, a prompter is expected to show the newcomers their A B C's, and keep the dance going on greased runners at the same time. His voice, too, must be clear and distinct (not necessarily deep in tone) and must penetrate the farthest corners of the hall. And, as if all of these qualities aren't enough, he must be a supreme showman: quick-witted and able to place a large, mixed crowd in position to dance in the minimum amount of time. With the floor directors usually dispensed with, it is up to the prompter to make all the floor arrangements.

Above all, the prompter must have supreme self-confidence, be a good politician, expert elocutionist, military strategist and a memorable master of ceremonies.

The best prompters baby their throats as if they were opera singers. Their greatest horror is laryngitis. They don't drink olive oil or wrap up in pink cotton batting, though; strange as it may seem, the oftener they call, the better their voice. They claim that six nights a week are better than one or two, because their vocal cords are really exercised then and so become stronger.

Always remember, then, that a good prompter is worth all he can get, and it is never a wise plan to start being thrifty by hiring a cheaper one. If you have one the crowd likes, move heaven and earth to keep him, because good callers can inspire the best in a dancer and make a good dancer even better.

Most good dancers in the old days were proud of their fancy steps, and some became famous for their particular brand. There was Jesse Spofford of Temple, New Hampshire, for instance, who invented the Cooper Step, and there was Joseph Barnes with his Brazing Step. These steps, High Betty Martin and the Double Shuffle, as well as lots of other showy figures, were performed to four bars of 2/4 or 6/8 time. Probably the most famous of all these is the Pigeon's Wing, a tremendously fast shake, first with the right and then with the left foot. And probably the most famous of all Pigeon's Wingers was Denman Thompson of *The Old Homestead*. No matter how dim the memory of the play, nobody can forget the scene of the kitchen junket. Here Denman could always guarantee a thunder of applause out of the most blasé house.

One reason for the decline in these steps is the fast tempo that the dance tunes are played in nowadays. Even Denman wouldn't have time today to do more than a clipped Pigeon's Wing, we're certain.

But while the present-day filigree-ers are less able to carry on their art, there still are countless anonymous ones who do their own individual steps that make you stop in your tracks to watch. As we said, all of those people dancing at the Springfield Fair were A-One showy dancers . . . what their names are, we are sorry we don't know.

But that's the way it is—the dancers are always the least exploited. Take Ralph Hale, Happy's brother, for instance. Probably nobody will ever hear of him outside of his little area but we can say that his "lame duck" step for the Morning Star must certainly deserve as much applause as the balconies gave old Denman. And what's more, the step seems to be original with Ralph.

Harry Frazier, too. We local neighbors admire Harry's grasshopper jump done in work-boots with a landing every bit as impressive as a smash on the kettle-drum. But Harry will doubtless never be seen behind the lights. Nor will Walter Hall with his one-foot pirouette ever gain more than local fame. Unless, of course, we have a booking agent come up some time to spend a weekend.

These men, and a lot more in every corner of New England, are the ones who are really writing our present-day chapter to the Country Dance Book. They are the ones who, without knowing it, are keeping the tradition alive.

And what, of all the traditions we have inherited and are trying to carry on, could be healthier, more blues-dispelling, or more fun? The answer is none. Strike up the band!

1976 note: Someone was listening. Country dance is alive in the land again.

The Music

SOME NOTES

We realize that you are not going to prop this book up on your piano and play directly from it. There are, however, plenty of books to be had which contain only music. These are far more practical and ample sources are given here.

However, the pieces of music you will find right in *The Country Dance Book*—Don't Let the Sap Boil Over, The Merry Dance, Small Potatoes and a Few in the Hill, Succotash Quadrille and Wild Goose Chase—are something pretty special, and at the time of the original edition unpublished as far as anyone knew.

SHEET MUSIC SOURCES

At the time of the 1937 edition the authors listed the following as good sources for country dance music: the Oliver Ditson Company and Walter Jacobs, Inc. of Boston; the Carl Fischer Music and Broadway Supply companies of New York City; the J. W. Pepper Company of Philadelphia and the E. T. Root Company of Homewood, Illinois. At the time they offered a wide collection of early square and contra dance tunes for fiddler and full orchestra alike.

Today, much of the above would no longer apply. Nonetheless there are plenty to turn to. For example, the Robbins Music Corporation (1775 Broadway, New York City) offers their collection of *200 Jigs, Reels and Country Dances,* among others.

Although the best jig, reel or hornpipe music has long

been available in general collections, the better quadrille, two-step, galop and polka music was, in earlier days, chiefly found in single sheet music form. This is no longer so sure; the book collection form seems to have won the day. Of special interest, perhaps, to readers of *The Country Dance Book* is *The Nelson Music Collection* published by the Rivercity Press of Rivercity, Massachusetts, 01337).

Other country dance collections are offered by Oak Publishers (39 West 60th Street, New York City) and by the Music Sales Company (33 West 60th Street, also New York City), to mention but two. In Canada, Gordon Thompson, Ltd. of Toronto is a good source. But perhaps the best source of all is the Country Dance and Song Society of 55 Christopher Street, New York City, 10014. They have a vast collection of both song and dance material—of all sorts and degrees of difficulty—and are happy to supply catalogs (and advice) on request. Readers should remember, too, that their local music store can help.

RECORD SOURCES

As for phonograph records, most music stores can give you a list almost as long as a wallflower's evening. But beware that on many of the commercial records the calls and music often fit western and southern dances better than those of New England. Be sure, when picking out records with calling in them, that the calls apply to the dances given in *The Country Dance Book*. Far better, select records with no dance directions: once you have studied the terms in Chapter II you will have no trouble in sensing the calls and changes in proper sequence.

Originally, for those partial to jigs, reels and hornpipes, the authors recommended writing *Irish Echoes,* a newspaper then published in Brooklyn (now moved to 3 East 48th Street, New York City, 10016). They offered such records for sale, and perhaps still do. Beyond that the authors suggested the records of the Decca and Victor companies.

Today, although modern square dance records are readily available, all country dance music is not always so easy to come by. Once more the reader will find his/her local music store of help. Much of this music is being put out by small independent companies such as the F & W and Green Mountain record companies, and the music store can direct the reader to them. But here again The Country Dance and Song Society is no doubt the best source. They have a full catalog of available country dance records of all sorts, speeds and price range.

THE TUNES THE DANCES ARE DANCED TO AND THE PAGES TO FIND THEM ON

Note: Appropriate tunes are given for all dances in the text. Some are danced to tunes of the same name; some are not. The tunes for dances danced to tunes of the same name, are marked with a ●

Country Dance Societies

As any reader of this book in 1976 must surely know, modern square dance activity has proliferated greatly across much of the United States and elsewhere this past half century. Almost every community seems to have at least one square dance club; some have more. Each state has its state-wide association; some several. The National Square Dance Convention (2936 Bella Vista, Midwest City, Oklahoma) alone has 20,000 members. There are publications exclusively for square dancers (*American Square Dance* of Sandusky, Ohio, for example) and any number of commercial ventures aimed at this market. There is even a Professional Square Dance Callers Association (330 Wadsworth Avenue, New York City).

It would, obviously, be impossible to list all the modern square dance clubs here. For those seeking information, a call to a local chamber of commerce, YMCA, or recreation department will surely put the reader in touch.

At the same time, interest in country dance of all sorts has grown and the number of country dance groups, and related organizations, along with it. There is, for example, the American Old-Time Fiddlers Association (6141 Morrill Avenue, Lincoln, Nebraska 68507), which not only prints fiddle music but arranges instruction and boasts over 4,000 members.

For those who wish to become actively involved we are indebted to the Country Dance and Song Society for the following list of almost 40 country dance and song centers across the country. For areas not touched by these centers, once again the reader should try his local chamber of commerce, YMCA (or YWCA), local recreation department, or perhaps the Cooperative Recreation Service (P.O. Box 333, Delaware, Ohio 43015).

COUNTRY DANCE SOCIETIES

ALABAMA

The Auburn Country Dance
Group
c/o Mr. and Mrs. P. H.
Hardie
1240 Hickory Lane
Auburn, AL 36830

ARIZONA

Folklanders
c/o Agnes Garner
Physical Ed. for Women
University of Arizona
Tucson, AR 85721

CALIFORNIA

The Carol Dancers
c/o Mary Judson
562 East Mendocino Street
Altadena, CA 91001

Hole in the Wall Country
Dancers
c/o Lew Bass
6575 Segovia Rd. #3
Isla Vista, CA 93017

San Diego Center
c/o Bruce Hamilton
1351 Reed Avenue #1
San Diego, CA 92109

San Francisco CDSS Center
c/o Nora Hughes
742 Union Street
San Francisco, CA 94133

ILLINOIS

Dunham Center of CDSS
c/o Mrs. P. S. Dickinson
River Bend Farm
St. Charles, IL 60174

University of Chicago Country Dancers
c/o Ida Noyes Hall
1212 East 59th Street
Chicago, IL 60637

INDIANA

Center for Traditional
Music and Dance
Dillon Bustin, Director
317 East Kirkwood Avenue
Bloomington, IN 47401

Earlham Country Dancers
Box E 1113
Earlham College
Richmond, IN 47374

French Lick Dancers
c/o Dillon Bustin
P.O. Box 309
French Lick, IN 47432

KENTUCKY

The Berea College Country
  Dancers
Mr. John Ramsay, Chairman
Box 287, Berea College
Berea, KY 40403

Berea CDSS Center
c/o Mrs. Wayne Berry
206 Jackson Street
Berea, KY 40403

Hindman Settlement School
  CDSS Center
c/o Lionel Duff
Hindman, KY 41822

Mountain Morris Men
c/o Peter Rogers
492 Bobolink Drive
Lexington, KY 40503

Western Ky. Univ. Center
c/o M. G. Karsner
Department of Physical Ed.
Western Kentucky Univ.
Bowling Green, KY 42101

MARYLAND

Baltimore-Washington
  CDSS Center
c/o Mrs. Joseph A. Blundon
9113 Wandering Trail Dr.
Potomac, MD 20854

Chesapeake Country Dancers
c/o Bob Dalsemer
44 East 26th Street
Baltimore, MD 21218

MASSACHUSETTS

Boston Center CDSS
57 Roseland Street
Somerville, MA 02143

MINNESOTA

Minneapolis English Coun-
  try Dancers
c/o Gwen Salisbury
215 Sheridan South
Minneapolis, MN 55405

MISSOURI

College Dance Department
c/o Miss Hariette Ann Gray
Stephens College
Columbia, MO 65201

NEW JERSEY

Ridgewood Center of CDSS
c/o Mrs. Mary Fassler
27 West Maple Avenue
Allendale, NJ 07401

NEW YORK

The Waldorf Country
  Dancers
c/o Mrs. Joan Carr
Waldorf Institute
Cambridge Avenue
Garden City, NY 11530

NORTH CAROLINA

Brasstown CDSS Center
Garnet Slone, Director
John C. Campbell Folk
    School
Brasstown, NC 28902

Kenilworth Kapers
c/o Mr. O. S. Clark
48 Sheridan Road
Asheville, NC 28803

PENNSYLVANIA

Country Dance Society of
    Pittsburgh
c/o Al Blank
107 Buckingham Road
Pittsburgh, PA 15215

Germantown Country
    Dancers
c/o Mrs. Morris Budnick
434 East Woodlawn
Philadelphia, PA 19144

Media Country Dancers
c/o Mrs. Richard Mont-
    gomery
213 S. Orange Street
Media, PA 19063

TENNESSEE

Knoxville Country Dancers
c/o Jonathan Sundell
Epworth Ministry
310 16th Street
Knoxville, TN 37916

Rutherford County Center
c/o Steve Cates
1417 Poplar Ave., Apt. A7
Murfreesboro, TN 37130

VERMONT

CDSS of Southeast Vermont
c/o Fred Breunig
40 High Street
Brattleboro, VT 05301

VIRGINIA

Albemarle Chapter of CDS
c/o John Wheeler
R.D. 4, Box 118
Charlottesville, VA 22902

Clinch Valley Country
    Dancers
c/o John McCutcheon
Clinch Valley College
Wise, VA 24293

English Country Dancers of
    Williamsburg
c/o Mr. and Mrs. L. Tucker
107 Indian Springs Road
Williamsburg, VA 23185

WASHINGTON

Leafield, c/o Steve Lane
510 11th Avenue E.
Seattle, WA 91802

WEST VIRGINIA

Capers Club
Peterstown High School
Peterstown, WV 24963

General Index

THE DANCES, STEPS, PEOPLE AND TERMS